AGAINST EMPIRE

Also published by City Lights

Contrary Notions: The Michael Parenti Reader

Superpatriotism

The Terrorism Trap: September 11 and Beyond

History as Mystery

America Besieged

Blackshirts & Reds: Rational Fascism and the Overthrow of Communism

Dirty Truths

AGAINST EMPIRE

Michael Parenti

CITY LIGHTS BOOKS
San Francisco

Cover design by John Miller, Big Fish Books
Cover art: Lawrence Ferlinghetti, *Unfinished Flag of the United States*
Book design by Nancy J. Peters
Typography by Harvest Graphics

Library of Congress Cataloging-in-Publication Data

Parenti, Michael, 1933–
    Against empire / Michael Parenti.
        p.   cm.
    ISBN 0-87286-298-4/ ISBN 13: 978-0-87286-298-2 : $12.95
    1. United States — Foreign relations — 1989–   I. Title.
E840.P265   1995
327.73—dc20   95-7481
                                                              CIP

Visit our web site: www.citylights.com

CITY LIGHTS BOOKS are edited by Lawrence Ferlinghetti and Nancy J. Peters and published at the City Lights Bookstore, 261 Columbus Avenue, San Francisco, CA 94133.

To Dewayne Holmes, a former Crips leader who brought peace between gangs in Los Angeles and who then became a community organizer fighting for democratic reforms in the inner city. For his efforts he was railroaded into prison on trumped-up charges and is serving seven years.

And to Theresa Allison, his valiant mother, who continues the struggle for social justice in her community and country.

ACKNOWLEDGMENTS

My heartfelt thanks to my valued friend Sally Soriano for her unwavering support and assistance in the writing of this book. Appreciation is also due to my research assistant Peggy Noton for her careful and crucial reading of the manuscript. A word of gratitude goes to my son, Christian Parenti, for furnishing me with useful sources and thoughtful criticisms. Kristin Nelson, Angela Bocage, and Ginger Walker also provided valuable assistance. Nancy J. Peters of City Lights Books provided an encouragement and enthusiasm that helped lighten my task, proving herself to be both a fine editor and good friend.

CONTENTS

CHAPTER 1

IMPERIALISM 101

Imperialism has been the most powerful force in world history over the last four or five centuries, carving up whole continents while oppressing indigenous peoples and obliterating entire civilizations. Yet, empire as it exists today is seldom accorded any serious attention by our academics, media commentators, and political leaders. When not ignored outright, the subject of imperialism has been sanitized, so that empires are called "commonwealths," and colonies become "territories" or "dominions." Imperialist military interventions become matters of "national defense," "national security," and maintaining "stability" in one or another region. In this book I want to look at imperialism for what it really is.

Across the Entire Globe

By "imperialism" I mean the process whereby the dominant politico-economic interests of one nation expropriate for their own enrichment the land, labor, raw materials, and markets of another people.

The earliest victims of Western European imperialism were other Europeans. Some eight hundred years ago, Ireland became the first colony of what later became known as the British Empire. Today, a part of Ireland still remains under British occupation. Other early Caucasian victims included the Eastern Europeans. The people Charlemagne worked to death in his mines in the early part of the ninth century were Slavs. So frequent and prolonged was the enslavement of Eastern Europeans that "Slav" became synonymous with servitude. Indeed, the word "slave" derives from "Slav." Eastern Europe was an early source of capital accumulation, having become wholly dependent upon Western manufactures by the seventeenth century.

A particularly pernicious example of intra-European imperialism was the Nazi aggression during World War II that gave the German business cartels and the Nazi state an opportunity to plunder the resources and exploit the labor of occupied Europe, including the slave labor of concentration camps.

The preponderant thrust of the European, North American, and Japanese imperial powers has been directed against Africa, Asia, and Latin America. By the nineteenth century, they saw the Third World as not only a source of raw materials and slaves but a market for manufactured goods. By the twentieth century, the industrial nations were exporting not only goods but capital, in the form of machinery, technology, investments, and loans. To say that we have entered the stage of capital export and investment is not to imply that the plunder of natural resources has ceased. If anything, the despoliation has accelerated.

Of the various notions about imperialism circulating today in the United States, the dominant one is that it no longer exists. Imperialism is not recognized as a legitimate concept, certainly not in regard to the United States. One may speak of "Soviet imperialism" or "nineteenth-century British imperialism" but not of *U.S.*

imperialism. A graduate student in political science at most universities in this country would not be granted the opportunity to research U.S. imperialism, on the grounds that such an undertaking would not be scholarly.[1] While many people throughout the world charge the United States with being an imperialist power, in this country people who talk of U.S. imperialism are usually judged to be mouthing ideological blather.

The Dynamic of Capital Expansion

Imperialism is older than capitalism. The Persian, Macedonian, Roman, and Mongol empires all existed centuries before the Rothschilds and Rockefellers. Emperors and conquistadors were interested mostly in plunder and tribute, gold and glory. Capitalist imperialism differs from these earlier forms in the way it systematically accumulates capital through the organized exploitation of labor and the penetration of overseas markets. Capitalist imperialism invests in other countries, dominating their economies, cultures, and political life, and integrating their productive structures into an international system of capital accumulation.

A central imperative of capitalism is expansion. Investors will not put their money into business ventures unless they can extract more than they invest. Increased earnings come only with growth in the enterprise. The capitalist ceaselessly searches for ways of making more money in order to make still more money. One must always invest to realize profits, gathering as much strength as possible in the face of competing forces and unpredictable markets.

Given its expansionist nature, capitalism has little inclination to stay home. Almost 150 years ago, Marx and Engels described a

---

1. Chapter 10 deals in more detail with the relationship between imperialism and academia.

bourgeoisie that "chases over the whole surface of the globe. It must nestle everywhere, settle everywhere, establish connections every-where. . . . It creates a world after its own image." The expansion-ists destroy whole societies. Self-sufficient peoples are forcibly transformed into disfranchised wage workers. Indigenous communi-ties and folk cultures are replaced by mass-market, mass-media, consumer societies. Cooperative lands are supplanted by agribusi-ness factory farms, villages by desolate shanty towns, autonomous regions by centralized autocracies.

Consider one of a thousand such instances. A few years ago the *Los Angeles Times* carried a special report on the rain forests of Borneo in the South Pacific. By their own testimony, the people there lived contented lives. They hunted, fished, and raised food in their jungle orchards and groves. But their entire way of life was ruthlessly wiped out by a few giant companies that destroyed the rain forest in order to harvest the hardwood for quick profits. Their lands were turned into ecological disaster areas and they themselves were transformed into disfranchised shantytown dwellers, forced to work for subsistence wages—when fortunate enough to find employment.

North American and European corporations have acquired con-trol of more than three-fourths of the known mineral resources of Asia, Africa, and Latin America. But the pursuit of natural resources is not the only reason for capitalist overseas expansion. There is the additional need to cut production costs and maximize profits by investing in countries with a plentiful supply of cheap labor. U.S. corporate foreign investment grew 84 percent from 1985 to 1990, with the most dramatic increase in cheap-labor countries like South Korea, Taiwan, Spain, and Singapore.

Because of low wages, low taxes, nonexistent work benefits, weak labor unions, and nonexistent occupational and environmental protections, U.S. corporate profit rates in the Third World are 50 percent greater than in developed countries. Citibank, one of the largest U.S. firms, earns about 75 percent of its profits from overseas operations. While profit margins at home sometimes have had a sluggish growth, earnings abroad have continued to rise dramatically, fostering the development of what has become known as the multinational or transnational corporation. Today some four hundred transnational companies control about 80 percent of the capital assets of the global free market and are extending their grasp into the ex-communist countries of Eastern Europe.

Transnationals have developed a global production line. General Motors has factories that produce cars, trucks, and a wide range of auto components in Canada, Brazil, Venezuela, Spain, Belgium, Yugoslavia, Nigeria, Singapore, Philippines, South Africa, South Korea, and a dozen other countries. Such "multiple sourcing" enables GM to ride out strikes in one country by stepping up production in another, playing workers of various nations against one other in order to discourage wage and benefit demands and undermine labor union strategies.

Not Necessary, Just Compelling

Some writers question whether imperialism is a necessary condition for capitalism, pointing out that most Western capital is invested in Western nations, not in the Third World. If corporations lost all their Third World investments, they argue, many of them could still survive on their European and North American markets. In response, one should note that capitalism might be able to survive without imperialism—but it shows no inclination to do so. It manifests no desire to discard its enormously profitable Third World enterprises. Imperialism may not be a necessary condition for investor survival but it seems to be an inherent tendency and a natural outgrowth of advanced capitalism. Imperial relations may not be the only way to pursue profits, but they are the most lucrative way.

Whether imperialism is necessary for capitalism is really not the question. Many things that are not absolutely necessary are still highly desirable, therefore strongly preferred and vigorously pursued. Overseas investors find the Third World's cheap labor, vital natural resources, and various other highly profitable conditions to be compellingly attractive. Superprofits may not be necessary for capitalism's survival but survival is not all that capitalists are interested in. Superprofits are strongly preferred to more modest earnings. That there may be no necessity between capitalism and imperialism does not mean there is no compelling linkage.

The same is true of other social dynamics. For instance, wealth does not necessarily have to lead to luxurious living. A higher portion of an owning class's riches could be used for investment rather than personal consumption. The very wealthy could survive on more modest sums but that is not how most of them prefer to live. Throughout history, wealthy classes generally have shown a preference for getting the best of everything. After all, the whole purpose of getting rich off other people's labor is to live well, avoiding all forms of thankless toil and drudgery, enjoying superior opportunities for lavish life-styles, medical care, education, travel, recreation, security, leisure, and opportunities for power and prestige. While none of these things are really "necessary," they are fervently clung to by those who possess them, as witnessed by the violent measures endorsed by advantaged classes whenever they feel the threat of an equalizing or leveling democratic force.

Myths of Underdevelopment

The impoverished lands of Asia, Africa, and Latin America are known to us as the "Third World," to distinguish them from the

"First World" of industrialized Europe and North America and the now largely defunct "Second World" of communist states. Third World poverty, called "underdevelopment," is treated by most Western observers as an original historic condition. We are asked to believe that it always existed, that poor countries are poor because their lands have always been infertile or their people unproductive.

In fact, the lands of Asia, Africa, and Latin America have long produced great treasures of foods, minerals, and other natural resources. That is why Europeans went through so much trouble to steal and plunder them. One does not go to poor places for self-enrichment. The Third World is rich. Only its people are poor—and it is because of the pillage they have endured.

The process of expropriating the natural resources of the Third World began centuries ago and continues to this day. First, the colonizers extracted gold, silver, furs, silks, and spices, then flax, hemp, timber, molasses, sugar, rum, rubber, tobacco, calico, cocoa, coffee, cotton, copper, coal, palm oil, tin, iron, ivory, ebony, and later on oil, zinc, manganese, mercury, platinum, cobalt, bauxite, aluminum, and uranium. Not to be overlooked is the most hellish of all expropriations: the abduction of millions of human beings into slave labor.

Through the centuries of colonization, many self-serving imperialist theories have been spun. I was taught in school that people in tropical lands are slothful and do not work as hard as we denizens of the temperate zone. In fact, the inhabitants of warm climates have performed remarkably productive feats, building magnificent civilizations well before Europe emerged from the Dark Ages. And today they often work long, hard hours for meager sums. Yet the early stereotype of the "lazy native" is still with us. In every capitalist society, the poor, both domestic and overseas, regularly are blamed for their own condition.

We hear that Third World peoples are culturally retarded in their attitudes, customs, and technical abilities. It is a convenient notion embraced by those who want to depict Western investments as a rescue operation designed to help backward peoples help themselves. This myth of "cultural backwardness" goes back to ancient times, used by conquerors to justify the enslavement of indigenous peoples. It was used by European colonizers over the last five centuries for the same purpose.

What cultural supremacy could be claimed by the Europeans of yore? From the fifteenth to nineteenth centuries Europe was "ahead" in such things as the number of hangings, murders, and other violent crimes; instances of venereal disease, smallpox, typhoid, tuberculosis, plagues, and other bodily afflictions; social inequality and poverty (both urban and rural); mistreatment of women and children; and frequency of famine, slavery, prostitution, piracy, religious massacre, and inquisitional torture. Those who believe the West has been the most advanced civilization should keep such "achievements" in mind.

More seriously, we might note that Europe enjoyed a telling advantage in navigation and armaments. Muskets and cannons, Gatling guns and gunboats, and today missiles, helicopter gunships, and fighter bombers have been the deciding factors when West meets East and North meets South. Superior firepower, not superior culture, has brought the Europeans and Euro–North Americans to positions of supremacy that today are still maintained by force, though not by force alone.

It was said that colonized peoples were biologically backward and less evolved than their colonizers. Their "savagery" and "lower" level of cultural evolution were emblematic of their inferior genetic evolution. But were they culturally inferior? In many parts of what is now considered the Third World, people developed impressive skills in architecture, horticulture, crafts, hunting, fishing, midwifery, medicine, and other such things. Their social customs were often far more gracious and humane and less autocratic and repressive than anything found in Europe at that time. Of course we must not romanticize these indigenous societies, some of which had a number of cruel and unusual practices of their own. But generally, their peoples enjoyed healthier, happier lives, with more leisure time, than did most of Europe's inhabitants.

Other theories enjoy wide currency. We hear that Third World poverty is due to overpopulation, too many people having too many children to feed. Actually, over the last several centuries, many Third World lands have been less densely populated than certain parts of Europe. India has fewer people per acre—but more poverty—than Holland, Wales, England, Japan, Italy, and a few other industrial countries. Furthermore, it is the industrialized nations of the First World, not the poor ones of the Third, that devour some 80 percent of the world's resources and pose the greatest threat to the planet's ecology.

This is not to deny that overpopulation is a real problem for the planet's ecosphere. Limiting population growth in all nations would help the global environment but it would not solve the problems of the poor—because overpopulation in itself is not the cause of poverty but one of its effects. The poor tend to have large families because children are a source of family labor and income and a support during old age.

Frances Moore Lappé and Rachel Schurman found that of seventy Third World countries, there were six—China, Sri Lanka, Colombia, Chile, Burma, and Cuba, and the state of Kerala in India —that had managed to lower their birth rates by one-third. They enjoyed neither dramatic industrial expansion nor high per capita incomes nor extensive family planning programs.[2] The factors they

---

2. The reference to China is prior to the 1979 modernization and rapid growth and prior to the one-child family program: see *Food First Development Report* no. 4, 1988.

had in common were public education and health care, a reduction of economic inequality, improvements in women's rights, food subsidies, and in some cases land reform. In other words, fertility rates were lowered not by capitalist investments and economic growth as such but by socio-economic betterment, even on a modest scale, accompanied by the emergence of women's rights.

Artificially Converted to Poverty

What is called "underdevelopment" is a set of social relations that has been forcefully imposed on countries. With the advent of the Western colonizers, the peoples of the Third World were actually set back in their development, sometimes for centuries. British imperialism in India provides an instructive example. In 1810, India was exporting more textiles to England than England was exporting to India. By 1830, the trade flow was reversed. The British had put up prohibitive tariff barriers to shut out Indian finished goods and were dumping their commodities in India, a practice backed by British gunboats and military force. Within a matter of years, the great textile centers of Dacca and Madras were turned into ghost towns. The Indians were sent back to the land to raise the cotton used in British textile factories. In effect, India was reduced to being a cow milked by British financiers.

By 1850, India's debt had grown to £53 million. From 1850 to 1900, its per capita income dropped by almost two-thirds. The value of the raw materials and commodities the Indians were obliged to send to Britain during most of the nineteenth century amounted yearly to more than the total income of the sixty million Indian agricultural and industrial workers. The massive poverty we associate with India was not that country's original historical condition. British imperialism did two things: first, it ended India's development, then it forcibly underdeveloped that country.

Similar bleeding processes occurred throughout the Third World. The enormous wealth extracted should remind us that there originally were few really poor nations. Countries like Brazil, Indonesia, Chile, Bolivia, Zaire, Mexico, Malaysia, and the Philippines were and in some cases still are rich in resources. Some lands have been so thoroughly plundered as to be desolate in all respects. However, most of the Third World is not "underdeveloped" but overexploited. Western colonization and investments have created a lower rather than a higher living standard.

Referring to what the English colonizers did to the Irish, Frederick Engels wrote in 1856: "How often have the Irish started out to achieve something, and every time they have been crushed politically and industrially. By consistent oppression they have been artificially converted into an utterly impoverished nation." So with most of the Third World. The Mayan Indians in Guatemala had a more nutritious and varied diet and better conditions of health in the early sixteenth century before the Europeans arrived than they have today. They had more craftspeople, architects, artisans, and horticulturists than today. What is called underdevelopment is a product of imperialism's superexploitation. Underdevelopment is itself a development.

Imperialism has created what I have termed "maldevelopment": modern office buildings and luxury hotels in the capital city instead of housing for the poor, cosmetic surgery clinics for the affluent instead of hospitals for workers, cash export crops for agribusiness instead of food for local markets, highways that go from the mines and latifundios to the refineries and ports instead of roads in the back country for those who might hope to see a doctor or a teacher.

Wealth is transferred from Third World peoples to the economic elites of Europe and North America (and more recently Japan) by direct plunder, by the expropriation of natural resources, the imposition of ruinous taxes and land rents, the payment of poverty wages, and the forced importation of finished goods at highly inflated prices. The colonized country is denied the freedom of trade and the opportunity to develop its own natural resources, markets, and industrial capacity. Self-sustenance and self-employment give way to wage labor. From 1970 to 1980, the number of wage workers in the Third World grew from 72 million to 120 million, and the rate is accelerating.

Hundreds of millions of Third World peoples now live in destitution in remote villages and congested urban slums, suffering hunger, disease, and illiteracy, often because the land they once tilled is now controlled by agribusiness firms that use it for mining or for commercial export crops such as coffee, sugar, and beef, instead of beans, rice, and corn for home consumption. A study of twenty of the poorest countries, compiled from official statistics, found that the number of people living in what is called "absolute poverty" or rock-bottom destitution, the poorest of the poor, is rising 70,000 a day and should reach 1.5 billion by the year 2000 (*San Francisco Examiner*, June 8, 1994).

Imperialism forces millions of children around the world to live nightmarish lives, their mental and physical health severely damaged by endless exploitation. A documentary film on the Discovery Channel (April 24, 1994) reported that in countries like Russia, Thailand, and the Philippines, large numbers of minors are sold into prostitution to help their desperate families survive. In countries like Mexico, India, Colombia, and Egypt, children are dragooned into health-shattering, dawn-to-dusk labor on farms and in factories and mines for pennies an hour, with no opportunity for play, schooling, or medical care.

In India, 55 million children are pressed into the work force. Tens of thousands labor in glass factories in temperatures as high as 100 degrees. In one plant, four-year-olds toil from five o'clock in the morning until the dead of night, inhaling fumes and contracting emphysema, tuberculosis, and other respiratory diseases. In the Philippines and Malaysia corporations have lobbied to drop age restrictions for labor recruitment. The pursuit of profit becomes a pursuit of evil.

Development Theory

When we say a country is "underdeveloped," we are implying that it is backward and retarded in some way, that its people have shown little capacity to achieve and evolve. The negative connotations of "underdeveloped" have caused the United Nations, the *Wall Street Journal*, and parties of various political persuasions to refer to Third World countries as "developing" nations, a term somewhat less insulting than "underdeveloped" but equally misleading. I prefer to use "Third World" because "developing" seems to be just a euphemistic way of saying "underdeveloped but belatedly starting to do something about it." It still implies that poverty was an original historic condition and not something imposed by imperialists. It also falsely suggests that these countries *are* developing when actually their economic conditions are usually worsening.

The dominant theory of the last half century, enunciated repeatedly by writers like Barbara Ward and W. W. Rostow and afforded wide currency, maintains that it is up to the rich nations of the North to help uplift the "backward" nations of the South, bringing them technology and proper work habits. This is an updated version of "the white man's burden," a favorite imperialist fantasy.

According to the development scenario, with the introduction of Western investments, workers in the poor nations will find more productive employment in the modern sector at higher wages. As capital accumulates, business will reinvest its profits, thus creating still more products, jobs, buying power, and markets. Eventually a more prosperous economy evolves.

This "development theory" or "modernization theory," as it is sometimes called, bears little relation to reality. What has emerged in the Third World is an intensely exploitive form of dependent capitalism. Economic conditions have worsened drastically with the growth of transnational corporate investment. The problem is not poor lands or unproductive populations but foreign exploitation and class inequality. Investors go into a country not to uplift it but to enrich themselves.

People in these countries do not need to be taught how to farm. They need the land and the implements to farm. They do not need to be taught how to fish. They need the boats and the nets and access to shore frontage, bays, and oceans. They need industrial plants to cease dumping toxic effusions into the waters. They do not need to be convinced that they should use hygienic standards. They do not need a Peace Corps volunteer to tell them to boil their water, especially when they cannot afford fuel or have no access to firewood. They need the conditions that will allow them to have clean drinking water and clean clothes and homes. They do not need advice about balanced diets from North Americans. They usually know what foods best serve their nutritional requirements. They need to be given back their land and labor so that they might work for themselves and grow food for their own consumption.

The legacy of imperial domination is not only misery and strife, but an economic structure dominated by a network of international corporations which themselves are beholden to parent companies based in North America, Europe, and Japan. If there is any harmonization or integration, it occurs among the global investor classes, not among the indigenous economies of these countries. Third World economies remain fragmented and unintegrated within themselves and among one another, both in the flow of capital and goods and in technology and organization. In sum, what we have is a world economy that has little to do with the economic needs of the world's people.

Neoimperialism: Skimming the Cream

Sometimes imperial domination is explained as arising from an innate desire for domination and expansion, a "territorial imperative." In fact, territorial imperialism is no longer the prevailing mode. Compared to the nineteenth and early twentieth centuries, when the European powers carved up the world among themselves, today there is almost no colonial dominion left. Colonel Blimp is dead and buried, replaced by men in business suits. Rather than being directly colonized by the imperial power, the weaker countries have been granted the trappings of sovereignty while Western finance capital retains control of the lion's share of their profitable resources. This relationship has gone under various names: "informal empire," "colonialism without colonies," "neocolonialism," and "neoimperialism."

U.S. political and business leaders were among the earliest practitioners of this new kind of empire, most notably in Cuba at the beginning of the twentieth century. Having forcibly wrested the island from Spain in the war of 1898, they eventually gave Cuba its formal independence. The Cubans now had their own government, constitution, flag, currency, and security force. But major foreign policy decisions remained in U.S. hands as did the island's wealth, including its sugar, tobacco, and tourist industries, and major imports and exports.

Historically U.S. capitalist interests have been less interested in acquiring more colonies than in acquiring more wealth, preferring to make off with the treasure of other nations without bothering to own and administer the nations themselves. Under neoimperialism, the flag stays home, while the dollar goes everywhere—frequently assisted by the sword.

After World War II, European powers like Britain and France adopted a strategy of neoimperialism. Financially depleted by years of warfare, and facing intensified popular resistance from within the Third World itself, they reluctantly decided that indirect economic hegemony was less costly and politically more expedient than outright colonial rule. They discovered that the removal of a conspicuously intrusive colonial rule made it more difficult for nationalist elements within the previously colonized countries to mobilize anti-imperialist sentiments.

Though the newly established government might be far from completely independent, it usually enjoyed more legitimacy in the eyes of its populace than a colonial administration controlled by the imperial power. Furthermore, under neoimperialism the native government takes up the costs of administering the country while the imperialist interests are free to concentrate on accumulating capital, which is all they really want to do.

After years of colonialism, the Third World country finds it extremely difficult to extricate itself from the unequal relationship with its former colonizer and impossible to depart from the global capitalist sphere. Those countries that try to make a break are subjected to punishing economic and military treatment by one or another major power, nowadays usually the United States.

The leaders of the new nations may voice revolutionary slogans, yet they find themselves locked into the global capitalist orbit, cooperating perforce with the First World nations for investment, trade, and aid. So we witnessed the curious phenomenon of leaders of newly independent Third World nations denouncing imperialism as the source of their countries' ills, while dissidents in these countries denounced these same leaders as collaborators of imperialism.

In many instances a comprador class emerged or was installed as a first condition for independence. A comprador class is one that cooperates in turning its own country into a client state for foreign interests. A client state is one that is open to investments on terms that are decidedly favorable to the foreign investors. In a client state, corporate investors enjoy direct subsidies and land grants, access to raw materials and cheap labor, light or nonexistent taxes, few effective labor unions, no minimum wage or child labor or occupational safety laws, and no consumer or environmental protections to speak of. The protective laws that do exist go largely unenforced.

In all, the Third World is something of a capitalist paradise, offering life as it was in Europe and the United States during the nineteenth century, with a rate of profit vastly higher than what might be earned today in a country with strong economic regulations. The comprador class is well recompensed for its cooperation. Its leaders enjoy opportunities to line their pockets with the foreign aid sent by the U.S. government. Stability is assured with the establishment of security forces, armed and trained by the United States in the latest technologies of terror and repression.

Still, neoimperialism carries risks. The achievement of de jure independence eventually fosters expectations of de facto independence. The forms of self rule incite a desire for the fruits of self rule. Sometimes a national leader emerges who is a patriot and reformer rather than a comprador collaborator. Therefore, the changeover from colonialism to neocolonialism is not without problems for the imperialists and represents a net gain for popular forces in the world.

CHAPTER 2

IMPERIAL DOMINATION UPDATED

In this chapter we will look at the major methods and effects of present-day imperial domination, including market and financial controls, foreign aid, political repression, and military violence—all of which leave a growing legacy of poverty and maldevelopment.

Market Inequality

The economy of Third World nations typically is concentrated on exporting a few raw materials or labor-intensive commodities. Since it is such a buyer's market, a poor nation finds itself in acute competition with other impoverished nations for the markets of more prosperous industrial countries. The latter are able to set trading terms that are highly favorable to themselves, playing one poor country off against another.

Attempts by Third World countries to overcome their vulnerability by forming trade cartels are usually unsuccessful, for they seldom are able to maintain a solid front, given their political differences, overall economic dependency, and lack of alternative markets. Trade among Third World countries themselves is increasingly retarded. In Africa, only about 6 percent of all international trade is among African countries—the rest is with European, Japanese, and North American firms.

Third World countries are underpaid for their exports and regularly overcharged for the goods they import from the industrial world. Thus, their coffee, cotton, meat, tin, copper, and oil are sold to foreign corporations at low prices in order to obtain—at painfully high prices—various manufactured goods, machinery, and spare parts. According to a former president of Venezuela, Carlos Andrés Perez: "This has resulted in a constant and growing outflow of capital and impoverishment of our countries."

Raw materials that are unavailable or in short supply in the United States are usually allowed into this country duty free, while goods that have been processed are subjected to tariffs. Thus coffee beans and raw timber are admitted with no charge, while processed coffee and sawed lumber face import duties. The industrial powers also prohibit the transfer of technology and credit to native-owned enterprises by threatening trade embargoes against Third World countries that have the temerity to develop an industrial product. Multinational corporations crowd out local businesses through superior financing, high-powered marketing, monopoly patents, and greater managerial resources. The more profitable the area of investment, the more likely is the local entrepreneur to be squeezed out by foreign investors.

Debt Domination

In many poor countries over half the manufacturing assets are owned or controlled by foreign companies. Even in instances when the multinationals have only a minority interest, they often retain a veto control. Even when the host nation owns the enterprise in its entirety, the multinationals will enjoy benefits through their near-monopoly of technology and international marketing. Such is the case with oil, an industry in which the giant companies own only about 38 percent of the world's crude petroleum production but control almost all the refining capacity and distribution.

Given these disadvantageous trade and investment relations, Third World nations have found it expedient to borrow heavily from Western banks and from the International Monetary Fund (IMF), which is controlled by the United States and other Western member-nations. By the 1990s, the Third World debt was approaching $2 trillion, an unpayable sum. The greater a nation's debt, the greater the pressure to borrow still more to meet deficits—often at still higher interest rates and on tighter payment terms.

An increasingly large portion of the earnings of indebted nations goes to servicing the debt, leaving still less for domestic consumption. The debts of some nations have grown so enormous that the interest accumulates faster than payments can be met. The debt develops a self-feeding momentum of its own, consuming more and more of the debtor nation's wealth.

By the late 1980s, in a country like Paraguay, 80 percent of export earnings went to pay the interest on foreign debt. Most debtor countries devote anywhere from one-third to two-thirds of their export earnings to servicing their debts. As early as 1983, the interest collected by foreign banks on Third World debts was three times higher than their profits from direct Third World investments.

To further exacerbate the problem, the national currencies of poorer nations are undervalued. As the economist Arjun Makhijani has noted, present exchange rates between prosperous and poor nations are not based on the comparative productivity of their labor forces and the domestic purchasing power of their currencies but are artificially pegged by the Western financial centers so as to undervalue the earnings of Third World inhabitants.

One might wish that the poorer nations would liberate themselves from this financial peonage by unilaterally canceling their debts. Fidel Castro urged them to do as much. But nations that default on their debts run the risk of being unable to qualify for short-term credit to fund imports. They risk having their overseas accounts frozen, their overseas assets seized, and their export markets closed.

To avoid default, the poor nations keep borrowing. But to qualify for more loans, a country must agree to the IMF's restructuring terms. It must cut back on domestic consumption while producing more for export in order to pay off more of the debt. The debtor nation must penalize its own population with cuts in food subsidies, housing, and other already insufficiently funded human services. It must devalue its currency, freeze wages, and raise prices so that its populace will work even harder and consume less. And it must offer generous tax concessions to foreign companies and eliminate subsidies to locally-owned and state-owned enterprises. Debt payments today represent a substantial net transfer of wealth from the working poor of the Third World to the coffers of international finance capital.

Foreign Aid as a Weapon

Most U.S. aid commits the recipient nation to buy U.S. goods at U.S. prices, to be transported in U.S. ships. In keeping with its commitment to capitalism, the U.S. government does not grant assistance to state-owned enterprises in Third World nations, only to the private sector. Most foreign aid never reaches the needy segments of the recipient nations. Much of it is used to subsidize U.S. corporate investment and a substantial amount finds its way into the coffers of corrupt comprador rulers. Some of it subsidizes the cash-crop exports of agribusiness at the expense of small farmers who grow food for local markets.

The net result of foreign aid, as with most overseas investment, is a greater concentration of wealth for the few and deeper poverty for the many. A large sum of money cannot be injected into a class society in a class-neutral way. It goes either to the rich or the poor, in most cases, the rich.

Aid is also a powerful means of political control. It is withheld when poorer nations dare to effect genuine reforms that might tamper with the distribution of wealth and power. Thus in 1970 when the democratically elected Allende government in Chile initiated reforms that benefited the working class and encroached upon the privileges of wealthy investors, all U.S. aid was cut off—except assistance to the Chilean military, which was increased. In some instances, aid is used deliberately to debilitate local production, as when Washington dumped sorghum and frozen chickens onto the Nicaraguan market to undercut cooperative farms and undermine land reform, or when it sent corn to Somalia to undercut local production and cripple independent village economies. It should be remembered that these corporate agricultural exports are themselves heavily subsidized by the U.S. government.

A key instrument of class-biased aid is the World Bank, an interlocking, international consortium of bankers and economists who spend billions of dollars—much of it from U.S. taxpayers—to finance projects that shore up repressive right-wing regimes and subsidize corporate investors at the expense of the poor and the environment. For instance, in the 1980s the World Bank built a highway into northwest Brazil's rain forests, then leveled millions of acres so that wealthy Brazilian ranchers could enjoy cheap grazing lands. Brazil also sent some of its urban poor down that highway to settle the land and further deplete it. Within ten years, the region was denuded and riddled with disease and poverty. As Jim Hightower put it: "All the world's bank robbers combined have not done one-tenth of one percent of the harm that the World Bank has in just fifty years."

With Rational Violence

Along with poverty and maldevelopment, the other legacy of imperialist economic domination is unspeakable political repression and state terror. In the history of imperialism there have been few if any peaceable colonizations. Only by establishing an overwhelming and often brutal military supremacy were the invaders able to take the lands of other peoples, extort tribute, undermine their cultures, destroy their townships, eliminate their crafts and industries, and indenture or enslave their labor. Such was done by the Spaniards in South and Central America; the Portuguese in Angola, Mozambique, and Brazil; the Belgians in the Congo; the Germans in Southwest Africa; the Italians in Libya, Ethiopia, and Somalia; the Dutch in the East Indies; the French in North Africa, Madagascar, and Indochina; the British in Ireland, China, India, Africa, and the Middle East; the Japanese in Korea, Manchuria, and China; and the Americans in North America (against Native Americans), the Philippines, Central America, the Caribbean, and Indochina. And this is hardly a complete listing.

Carving up the world has often been treated by the apologists of imperialism as a natural phenomenon, involving an "international specialization of production." In fact, what is distinct about imperialism is its highly *un*natural quality, its repeated reliance upon armed coercion and repression. Empires do not emerge naturally and innocently "in a fit of absentmindedness," as was said of the British Empire. They are welded together with deliberate deceit, greed, and ruthless violence. They are built upon the sword, the whip, and the gun. The history of imperialism is about the enslavement and slaughter of millions of innocents, a history no less dreadful for remaining conveniently untaught in most of our schools.

Terror remains one of the common instruments of imperialist domination. With the financial and technical assistance of the U.S. Central Intelligence Agency (CIA) and other such units, military and security police throughout various client states are schooled in the fine arts of surveillance, interrogation, torture, intimidation, and assassination. The U.S. Army School of the Americas (SOA) at Fort Benning, Georgia, known throughout Latin America as the "School of Assassins," trains military officers from U.S. client states in the latest methods of repression. In a country like El Salvador, a majority of the officers implicated in village massacres and other atrocities are SOA graduates.

The comprador repressors have forced victims to witness the torture of friends and relatives, including children. They have raped women in the presence of family members, burned sexual organs with acid or scalding water, placed rats in women's vaginas and into the mouths of prisoners, and mutilated, punctured, and cut off various parts of victims' bodies, including genitalia, eyes, and tongues. They have injected air into women's breasts and into veins, causing slow painful death, shoved bayonets and clubs into the vagina or, in the case of men, into the anus causing rupture and death.[1]

In countries that have had anticapitalist revolutionary governments, which redistributed economic resources to the many rather than the few, such as Nicaragua, Mozambique, Angola, and Afghanistan, the U.S. national security state has supported antigovernment mercenary forces in wars of attrition that destroy schools, farm cooperatives, health clinics, and whole villages. Women and girls are raped and tens of thousands are maimed, murdered, or psychologically shattered. Thousands of young boys are kidnapped and conscripted into the U.S.-backed counterrevolutionary forces.

---

1. I offer more detailed and documented instances in my *The Sword and the Dollar; Imperialism, Revolution, and the Arms Race.* New York: St. Martin's Press, 1988).

Millions of citizens are deracinated, ending in refugee camps. These wars of attrition extract a horrific toll on human life and eventually force the revolutionary government to discard its programs.

In procapitalist countries like El Salvador and Guatemala, the U.S. national security state is on the side of the government, rendering indispensable counterinsurgency assistance in order to suppress popular liberation forces. By the "U.S. national security state" I mean to the Executive Office of the White House, the National Security Council (NSC), National Security Administration, Central Intelligence Agency, Pentagon, Federal Bureau of Investigation, and other such units that are engaged in surveillance, suppression, covert action, and forceful interventions abroad and at home.

The protracted war waged against the people of El Salvador is one of many tragic examples of U.S.-backed counterinsurgency against people fighting for social justice. U.S.-trained and equipped Salvadoran troops massacred, as at El Mozote, whole villages suspected of being sympathetic to the guerrillas. Between 1978 and 1994 some 70,000 Salvadorans had been killed, mostly by government forces. Some 540,000 had fled into exile. Another quarter of a million were displaced or forced into resettlement camps by the military. All this in a country of only four million people.

In neighboring Guatemala, the loss of life due to the CIA-sponsored thirty-five-year-old conflict was estimated at 100,000 by 1994, with an additional 60,000 disappeared. Some 440 villages suspected of sympathizing with the guerrillas have been destroyed and most of their residents massacred. Almost a million people have fled the country and another million have become internal migrants, forced from their homes in widespread counterinsurgency actions. The killings continue.

In Colombia, thousands were murdered by government forces in a long guerrilla war. In the years of armistice that followed, more than a thousand anticapitalist or reformist politicians and activists were killed by right-wing paramilitary groups, including two presidential candidates of the Patriotic Union and a member of the Colombian Senate who was head of the Communist party. The killings continue there also—without a murmur of protest from the United States, which continues to send military aid to Colombia.

In Indonesia, the U.S.-backed military killed anywhere from 500,000 to one million people in 1965, destroying the Indonesian Communist party and most of its suspected sympathizers in what even the *New York Times* (March 12, 1966) called "one of the most savage mass slaughters of modern political history." Ten years later, the same Indonesian military invaded East Timor, overthrew its reformist government and killed between 100,000 and 200,000 out of a population of about 600,000. The aggression was launched the day after President Gerald Ford and Secretary of State Henry Kissinger concluded a visit to Indonesia. Philip Liechty, a CIA official there at the time, recently commented (*New York Times*, August 12, 1994) that General Soeharto of Indonesia "was explicitly given the green light to do what he did." Liechty noted that most of the weapons used by the Indonesian military, as well as ammunition and food, were from the United States.

Military force is in even greater evidence today than during the era of colonial conquest and occupation. The United States maintains the most powerful military machine on earth. Its supposed purpose was to protect democracy from communist aggression, but the U.S. military's actual mission—as demonstrated in Vietnam, Cambodia, Laos, Lebanon, the Dominican Republic, Grenada, and Panama—has been not to ward off Russian or Cuban invasions but to prevent indigenous anticapitalist, revolutionary or populist-nationalist governments from prevailing.

U.S. military force is also applied indirectly, by sponsoring Third

World armies, gendarmerie, and intelligence and security units—including death squads. Their purpose is not to safeguard their autocratic governments from a nonexistent communist invasion but to suppress and terrorize rebellious elements within their own populations or in adjacent countries—as Morocco does in the Western Sahara and Indonesia in East Timor.

In addition to financing Third World counterintelligence and internal security forces, the U.S. government is involved in advancing and upscaling the military forces of a dozen or so client-state nations, including South Korea, Turkey, Indonesia, Argentina, and Taiwan, with jet fighters, helicopter gunships, tanks, armored fighting vehicles, artillery systems, frigates, and guided missiles.

The planners and practitioners of imperialism find it necessary to resort to extreme measures of coercion in order to implement their policies of politico-economic domination. The disreputable henchmen, enlisted to do the actual dirty work of assassination and torture, are not born sadists and executioners. They are trained in the necessary techniques by their CIA advisers. Government torturers in Latin America themselves have stated that they are "professionals," whose task is to elicit information from *subversivos*, so as better to prosecute the war against them. Likewise, death squads do not kill people in random frenzies. They carefully target political opponents, labor leaders, student protestors, reform-minded clergy, and journalists who get too critical.

Of course, the CIA personnel who devise these violent programs do not consider themselves involved in anything less noble than the defense of U.S. interests abroad. They may admit that certain of their methods are unsavory but they are quick to point out the necessity of fighting fire with fire, emphasizing that a communist victory is a far greater evil than whatever repressive expediencies they are compelled to utilize. So they justify their crimes by saying that their victims are criminals. The national security warriors do not support torturers and death squads arbitrarily, but as part of a process of extermination and repression in defense of specific politico-economic interests.

Imperialism must build a state-supported security system to safeguard private overseas interests. Sometimes the state stakes out a claim on behalf of private interests well before investors are prepared to do so for themselves. Almost a century ago, President Woodrow Wilson made this clear when he observed that the government "must open these [overseas] gates of trade, and open them wide, open them before it is altogether profitable to open them, or altogether reasonable to ask private capital to open them at a venture."

The state must protect not only the overseas investments of particular firms but the entire capital accumulation process itself. This entails the systematic suppression of revolutionary and populist-nationalist movements that seek to build alternative economic systems along more egalitarian, collectivist lines.

Low Intensity Imperialism

It was with domestic opinion in mind that the U.S. imperialists developed the method of "low intensity conflict" to wreak death and destruction upon countries or guerrilla movements that pursued an alternative course of development. This approach recognizes that Third World guerrilla forces have seldom, if ever, been able to achieve all-out military victory over the occupying army of an industrial power or its comprador army. The best the guerrillas can hope to do is wage a war of attrition, depriving the imperialist country of a final victory, until the latter's own population grows weary of the costs and begins to challenge the overseas commitment. The war then becomes *politically* too costly for the imperialists to prosecute.

The national liberation resistance in Algeria never came close to defeating the French, yet it prevailed long enough to cause the Fourth Republic to fall and force France to concede independence. The wars that Portugal waged in Guinea-Bissau, Angola, and Mozambique proved so protracted and costly that the Salazar dictatorship was destabilized and eventually overthrown. In the United States, the seemingly endless Vietnam War caused the country to be torn by mass demonstrations, sit-ins, riots, draft evasion, and other radicalizing acts of resistance.

To avoid stirring up such political opposition at home, Washington policymakers have developed the technique of low intensity conflict, a mode of warfare that avoids all-out, high-visibility, military engagements and thereby minimizes the use and loss of U.S. military personnel. A low-intensity war is a proxy war, using the mercenary troops of the U.S.-backed Third World government. With Washington providing military trainers and advisers, superior firepower, surveillance and communications assistance, and generous funds, these forces are able to persist indefinitely, destroying a little at a time, with quick sorties into the countryside and death-squad assassinations in the cities and villages. They forgo an all-out sweep against guerrilla forces that is likely to fall short of victory and invite criticism of its futility and savagery.

The war pursued by the Reagan and Bush administrations against Nicaragua was prosecuted for almost a decade. The counterinsurgency war in El Salvador lasted over fifteen years; in the Philippines over twenty years; in Colombia, over thirty years; and in Guatemala, thirty-five years. Once low-intensity conflict is adopted there are no more big massacres, no massive military engagements, no dramatic victories or dramatic setbacks, no Dienbienphu or Tet Offensive.

The U.S. public is not galvanized to opposition because not much seems to be happening and the intervention drops from the news.

Like the guerrillas themselves, the interventionists pursue a war of attrition but *against* the people rather than with their support. Their purpose is to demonstrate that they have endless time and resources, that they will be able to outlast the guerrilla forces not only militarily, but also politically, because there is now scant pressure for withdrawal from their own populace back home.

At the same time, the guerrilla force cannot exist without the support of its own people, who themselves become increasingly demoralized by the human costs of the conflict. The growing war weariness of the Salvadoran people was one of the considerations that led the FMLN liberation forces to risk a negotiated peace with a treacherous Salvadoran government and its U.S. sponsors.

The Guatemalan and Salvadoran guerrillas were never completely defeated but they were militarily contained, leaving them in an increasingly difficult political situation. Even when the FMLN demonstrated with diminishing frequency that it still had the ability to launch attacks, the outcome was of limited military significance and often costly. With low-intensity conflict, guerrilla forces experience the loss of their greatest strategic weapon: the ability to sustain greater losses for a longer time than can the imperialists, the ability to outlast them politically. But now the imperialist forces can remain in the field indefinitely. Low-intensity warfare is as much a political strategy as a military one.

In Nicaragua, Mozambique, Angola, Ethiopia, Afghanistan, and other countries, the imperialist intervention consisted not of a government counterinsurgency against guerrillas but a brutal campaign by U.S.-backed mercenary forces against the "soft targets" of an aspiring revolutionary society, the rural clinics, towns, cooperative farms, and the vulnerable, poorly defended population. The targeted populace is bled and battered until it feels it can take no more. The cry for peace comes not from the people in the imperialist country but from the people in the victimized land, who eventually are forced to submit to their batterers' economic and political agenda.

Globalization by GATT

Among the recent undertakings by politico-economic elites are the North American Free Trade Agreement (NAFTA) and the 1993 Uruguayan Round of the General Agreement on Tariffs and Trade (GATT), which represent attempts to circumvent the sovereignty of nation-states in favor of the transnational corporations. As presented to the public, NAFTA and GATT will break down tariff walls, integrate national economies into a global system, and benefit the peoples of all nations with increased trade. This "globalization" process is treated as a benign and natural historical development that supposedly has taken us from regional to national and now to international market relations.

The goal of the transnational corporation is to become truly transnational, poised above the sovereign power of any particular nation, while being serviced by the sovereign powers of all nations. A decade ago, General Motors announced it was a global company, rather than merely an American one, because of its investments around the world. As if to bring the point home, GM continued to close its stateside factories and open new ones abroad. In a similar spirit, Cyril Siewert, chief financial officer of Colgate Palmolive Company, was quoted in the *New York Times* (May 21, 1989) as saying, "The United States doesn't have an automatic call on our [corporation's] resources. There is no mindset that puts this country first." Years ago, Dow Chemical admitted it had been thinking of becoming an *anational* firm, one that had no allegiance—and therefore no obligations or accountability—to any country. Dow was considering buying a Caribbean island and chartering itself to the island as a power unto itself.

With GATT, there will be no need for corporate island kingdoms. The corporate power will be elevated above the sovereign powers of all nation states. The GATT agreements create a World Trade Organization (WTO), an international association of over 120 signatory nations, with the same legal status as the United Nations. WTO has the authority to prevent, overrule, or dilute the environmental, social, consumer, and labor laws of any nation. It sets up panels composed of nonelected trade specialists who act as judges over economic issues, placing them beyond the reach of national sovereignty and popular control, thereby ensuring that community interests will be subordinated to finance capital.

Confirmed by no elective body and limited by no conflict-of-interest provisions, these panelists can have financial stakes in the very issues they adjudicate. They meet in secret, do not publicize their proceedings, and are not subject to administrative appeal. Their function is to create a world in which the only regulators and producers are the transnational corporations themselves. As Kim Moody observes (*Labor Notes*, February 1944), GATT's 500 pages of rules are not directed against business trade and investment but against governments. Signatory governments must lower tariffs, end farm subsidies, treat foreign companies the same as domestic ones, honor all corporate patent claims, and obey the rulings of a permanent elite bureaucracy, the WTO. Should a country refuse to change its laws when a WTO panel so dictates, GATT can impose international trade sanctions, depriving the resistant country of needed markets and materials. GATT will benefit strong nations at the expense of weaker ones, and rich interests at the expense of the rest of us.

Under GATT, some countries have already argued that mandatory nutritional labeling on food products, marine-life protection laws, fuel economy and emission standards for cars, the ban on asbestos, the ban on import products made by child labor, and the ban on endangered-species products and on dangerous pesticides constitute "unfair non-tariff trade barriers." Citizens acting at the local, state, and national levels have become something of a hindrance to corporations acting at the global level. In a June 1994 statement, Ralph Nader noted that the WTO "would greatly reduce citizen involvement in matters of commerce," undermining present U.S. regulatory laws by circumventing what little popular sovereignty we have been able to achieve.

Under the guise of protecting "intellectual property rights," GATT allows multinationals to impose compulsory licensing and monopoly property rights on indigenous and communal agriculture. In this way GATT strengthens corporate ability to penetrate locally self-sufficient communities and monopolize their resources. Nader gives the example of the neem tree, whose extracts contain natural pesticidal, medicinal, and other valuable properties. Cultivated for centuries in India, the tree has attracted the attention of various pharmaceutical companies, who have started filing monopoly patents, causing mass protests by Indian farmers. Armed with the patents, as legislated by the WTO, the pharmaceuticals will gain monopoly control over the marketing of neem tree products.

Generally, GATT advances the massive corporate acquisition of publicly owned property and the holdings of local owners and worker collectives. Deprived of tariff protections, many small family farms in North America and Europe will go under, and the self-sufficient village agricultural economies of much of Asia and Africa will be destroyed. As Kim Moody notes, "Third World peasant producers will be driven from the land by the millions, as is already happening in Mexico [under NAFTA]."

We are told that to remain competitive under GATT, we in North America will have to increase our productivity while reducing our labor and production costs. We will have to spend less on social services and introduce more wage concessions, more restructuring, deregulation, and privatization. Only then might we cope with the impersonal forces sweeping us along. In fact, there is nothing impersonal about these forces. GATT was consciously planned by business and governmental elites over a period of years, by interests that have explicitly pursued a deregulated world economy and have opposed all democratic checks upon business practices.

As capital becomes ever more mobile and unaccountable under plans like NAFTA and GATT, the people of any one province, state, or nation will find it increasingly difficult to get their government to impose protective regulations or develop new forms of public sector production. To offer one instance: Under the free-trade agreements between Canada and the United States, the single-payer auto insurance program adopted by the province of Ontario was declared "unfair competition" by U.S. insurance companies. The citizens of Ontario were not allowed to exercise their sovereign power to institute an alternative not-for-profit insurance system.

Over the last two decades, in Latin America, Asia, and even in Europe and North America, conservative forces have pushed hard to take publicly owned not-for-profit industries and services (mines, factories, oil wells, banks, railroads, telephone companies, utilities, television systems, postal services, health care, and insurance firms) and sell them off at bargain prices to private interests to be operated for profit.

In India, as in a few other countries, nationally oriented leaders attempted with some success to push out Western companies, exclude foreign investors from its stock exchanges, build up the public sector, and create homemade consumer goods for local markets. India's economic links with the Soviet Union bolstered such efforts. But with the collapse of the USSR, the advent of GATT, and a newly installed conservative government in New Delhi, India is headed for recolonization. By the early 1990s, previously excluded western companies like Coca-Cola had returned; Western investments were surging; entire industries and consumer markets were once more completely under foreign control; and government-owned industries were being privatized, against the protests of their employees and with inevitable cuts in wages and jobs. A similar process is taking place in the Eastern European countries whose economies had been heavily subsidized by the Soviet Union.

Designed to leave the world's economic destiny to the tender mercy of bankers and multinational corporations, globalization is a logical extension of imperialism, a victory of empire over republic, international finance capital over democracy.

CHAPTER 3

INTERVENTION:
WHOSE GAIN? WHOSE PAIN?

Today, the United States is the foremost proponent of recolonization and leading antagonist of revolutionary change throughout the world. Emerging from World War II relatively unscathed and superior to all other industrial countries in wealth, productive capacity, and armed might, the United States became the prime purveyor and guardian of global capitalism. Judging by the size of its financial investments and military force, judging by every imperialist standard except direct colonization, the U.S. empire is the most formidable in history, far greater than Great Britain in the nineteenth century or Rome during antiquity.

A Global Military Empire

The exercise of U.S. power is intended to preserve not only the international capitalist system but U.S. hegemony of that system. The Pentagon's "Defense Planning Guidance" draft (1992) urges the United States to continue to dominate the international system by "discouraging the advanced industrialized nations from challenging our leadership or even aspiring to a larger global or regional role." By maintaining this dominance, the Pentagon analysts assert, the United States can ensure "a *market-oriented* zone of peace and prosperity that encompasses more than two-thirds of the world's economy" [italics added].

This global power is immensely costly. Today, the United States spends more on military arms and other forms of "national security" than the rest of the world combined. U.S. leaders preside over a global military apparatus of a magnitude never before seen in human history. In 1993 it included almost a half-million troops stationed at over 395 major military bases and hundreds of minor installations in thirty-five foreign countries, and a fleet larger in total tonnage and firepower than all the other navies of the world combined, consisting of missile cruisers, nuclear submarines, nuclear aircraft carriers, destroyers, and spy ships that sail every ocean and make port on every continent. U.S. bomber squadrons and long-range missiles can reach any target, carrying enough explosive force to destroy entire countries with an overkill capacity of more than 8,000 strategic nuclear weapons and 22,000 tactical ones. U.S. rapid deployment forces have a firepower in conventional weaponry vastly superior to any other nation's, with an ability to slaughter with impunity, as the massacre of Iraq demonstrated in 1990–91.

Since World War II, the U.S. government has given over $200 billion in military aid to train, equip, and subsidize more than 2.3 million troops and internal security forces in some eighty countries, the purpose being not to defend them from outside invasions but to protect ruling oligarchs and multinational corporate investors from the dangers of domestic anticapitalist insurgency. Among the recipients have been some of the most notorious military autocracies in history, countries that have tortured, killed, or otherwise maltreated large numbers of their citizens because of their dissenting political views, as in Turkey, Zaire, Chad, Pakistan, Morocco, Indonesia, Honduras, Peru, Colombia, El Salvador, Haiti, Cuba (under Batista), Nicaragua (under Somoza), Iran (under the Shah), the Philippines (under Marcos), and Portugal (under Salazar).

U.S. leaders profess a dedication to democracy. Yet over the past five decades, democratically elected reformist governments in Guatemala, Guyana, the Dominican Republic, Brazil, Chile, Uruguay, Syria, Indonesia (under Sukarno), Greece, Argentina, Bolivia, Haiti, and numerous other nations were overthrown by pro-capitalist militaries that were funded and aided by the U.S. national security state.

The U.S. national security state has participated in covert actions or proxy mercenary wars against revolutionary governments in Cuba, Angola, Mozambique, Ethiopia, Portugal, Nicaragua, Cambodia, East Timor, Western Sahara, and elsewhere, usually with dreadful devastation and loss of life for the indigenous populations. Hostile actions also have been directed against reformist governments in Egypt, Lebanon, Peru, Iran, Syria, Zaire, Jamaica, South Yemen, the Fiji Islands, and elsewhere.

Since World War II, U.S. forces have directly invaded or launched aerial attacks against Vietnam, the Dominican Republic, North Korea, Laos, Cambodia, Lebanon, Grenada, Panama, Libya, Iraq, and Somalia, sowing varying degrees of death and destruction.

Before World War II, U.S. military forces waged a bloody and protracted war of conquest in the Philippines from 1899 to 1903. Along with fourteen other capitalist nations, the United States invaded and occupied parts of socialist Russia from 1918 to 1921. U.S. expeditionary forces fought in China along with other Western armies to suppress the Boxer Rebellion and keep the Chinese under the heel of European and North American colonizers. U.S. Marines invaded and occupied Nicaragua in 1912 and again from 1926 to

1933; Haiti, from 1915 to 1934; Cuba, from 1898 to 1902; Mexico, in 1914 and 1916. There were six invasions of Honduras between 1911 to 1925; Panama was occupied between 1903 and 1914.

Why Intervention?

Why has a professedly peace-loving, democratic nation found it necessary to use so much violence and repression against so many peoples in so many places? An important goal of U.S. policy is to make the world safe for the *Fortune* 500 and its global system of capital accumulation. Governments that strive for any kind of economic independence or any sort of populist redistributive politics, that attempt to take some of their economic surplus and apply it to not-for-profit services that benefit the people—such governments are the ones most likely to feel the wrath of U.S. intervention or invasion.

The designated "enemy" can be a reformist, populist, military government as in Panama under Torrijo (and even under Noriega), Egypt under Nasser, Peru under Velasco, and Portugal after Salazar; a Christian socialist government as in Nicaragua under the Sandinistas; a social democracy as in Chile under Allende, Jamaica under Manley, Greece under Papandreou, and the Dominican Republic under Bosch; a Marxist-Leninist government as in Cuba, Vietnam, and North Korea; an Islamic revolutionary order as in Libya under Qaddafi; or even a conservative militarist regime as in Iraq under Saddam Hussein, if it should get out of line on oil prices and oil quotas.

The public record shows that the United States is the foremost interventionist power in the world. There are varied and overlapping reasons for this:

Protect Direct Investments. In 1907, Woodrow Wilson recognized the support role played by the capitalist state on behalf of private capital:

Since trade ignores national boundaries and the manufacturer insists on having the world as a market, the flag
of his nation must follow him, and the doors of the
nations which are closed against him must be battered
down. Concessions obtained by financiers must be safe-
guarded by ministers of state, even if the sovereignty of
unwilling nations be outraged in the process. Colonies
must be obtained or planted, in order that no useful corner of the world may be overlooked or left unused.

Later, as president of the United States, Wilson noted that the
United States was involved in a struggle to "command the economic
fortunes of the world."

During the late nineteenth and early twentieth centuries, large
U.S. investments in Central America and the Caribbean brought frequent military intercession, protracted war, prolonged occupation, or
even direct territorial acquisition, as with Hawaii, Puerto Rico, and
the Panama Canal Zone. The investments were often in the natural
resources of the country: sugar, tobacco, cotton, and precious metals. In large part, the interventions in the Gulf in 1991 (see Chapter
6) and in Somalia in 1993 (Chapter 7) were respectively to protect
oil profits and oil prospects.

In the post–Cold War era, Admiral Charles Larson noted that,
although U.S. military forces have been reduced in some parts of the
world, they remain at impressive levels in the Asia-Pacific area
because U.S. trade in that region is greater than with either Europe or
Latin America. Naval expert Charles Meconis also pointed to "the
economic importance of the region" as the reason for a major U.S. military presence in the Pacific (see Daniel Schirmer, *Monthly Review*,
July/August 1994). In these instances, the sword follows the dollar.

Create Opportunities for New Investments. Sometimes the dollar
follows the sword, as when military power creates opportunities for

new investments. Thus, in 1915, U.S. leaders, citing "political insta-
bility," invaded Haiti and crushed the popular militia. The troops
stayed for nineteen years. During that period French, German, and
British investors were pushed out and U.S. firms tripled their investments in Haiti.

More recently, Taiwanese companies gave preference to U.S.
firms over those from Japan because the U.S. military was protecting Taiwan. In 1993, Saudi Arabia signed a $6 billion contract for jet
airliners exclusively with U.S. companies. Having been frozen out of
the deal, a European consortium charged that Washington had pressured the Saudis, who had become reliant on Washington for their
military security in the post–Gulf War era.

*Preserving Politico-Economic Domination and the Capital
Accumulation System.* Specific investments are not the only imperialist concern. There is the overall commitment to safeguarding the
global class system, keeping the world's land, labor, natural
resources, and markets accessible to transnational investors. More
important than particular holdings is the whole *process* of investment and profit. To defend that process the imperialist state thwarts
and crushes those popular movements that attempt any kind of redistributive politics, sending a message to them and others that if they
try to better themselves by infringing upon the prerogatives of corporate capital, they will pay a severe price.

In two of the most notable U.S. military interventions, Soviet
Russia from 1918 to 1920 and Vietnam from 1954 to 1973, most of
the investments were European, not American. In these and other
such instances, the intent was to prevent the emergence of competing social orders and obliterate all workable alternatives to the capitalist client-state. That remains the goal to this day, the countries
most recently targeted being South Yemen, North Korea, and Cuba.

Ronald Reagan was right when he avowed that his invasion of

Grenada was not to protect the U.S. nutmeg supply. There was plenty of nutmeg to be got from Africa. He was acknowledging that Grenada's natural resources were not crucial. Nor would the revolutionary collectivization of a poor nation of 102,000 souls represent much of a threat or investment loss to global capitalism. But if enough countries follow that course, it eventually would put the global capitalist system at risk.

Reagan's invasion of Grenada served notice to all other Caribbean countries that this was the fate that awaited any nation that sought to get out from under its client-state status. So the invaders put an end to the New Jewel Movement's revolutionary programs for land reform, health care, education, and cooperatives. Today, with its unemployment at new heights and its poverty at new depths, Grenada is once again firmly bound to the free market world. Everyone else in the region indeed has taken note.

The imperialist state's first concern is not to protect the direct investments of any particular company, although it sometimes does that, but to protect the global system of private accumulation from competing systems. The case of Cuba illustrates this point. It has been pointed out that Washington's embargo against Cuba is shutting out U.S. business from billions of dollars of attractive investment and trade opportunities. From this it is mistakenly concluded that U.S. policy is not propelled by economic interests. In fact, it demonstrates just the opposite, an unwillingness to tolerate those states that try to free themselves from the global capitalist system.

The purpose of the capitalist state is to do things for the advancement of the entire capitalist system that individual corporate interests cannot do. Left to their own competitive devices, business firms are not willing to abide by certain unwritten rules of common systemic interest. This is true within both the domestic economy and in foreign ventures. Like any good capitalist organization, a business firm may have a general long-range interest in seeing Cuban socialism crushed, but it might have a more tempting immediate interest in doing a profitable business with the class enemy. It remains for the state to force individual companies back in line.[1] What is at stake is not the investments within a particular Third World country but the long-range security of the entire system of transnational investment. No country that pursues an independent course of development shall be allowed to prevail as a dangerous example to other nations.

Common Confusions

Some critics have argued that economic factors have not exerted an important influence on U.S. interventionist policy because most interventions are in countries that have no great natural treasures and no large U.S. investments, such as Grenada, El Salvador, Nicaragua, and Vietnam. This is like saying that police are not especially concerned about protecting wealth and property because most of their forceful actions take place in poor neighborhoods. Interventionist forces do not go where capital exists as such; they go where capital is threatened. They have not intervened in affluent Switzerland, for instance, because capitalism in that country is relatively secure and unchallenged. But if leftist parties gained power in Bern and attempted to nationalize Swiss banks and major properties, it very likely would invite the strenuous attentions of the Western industrial powers.

Some observers maintain that intervention is bred by the national-security apparatus itself, the State Department, the National Security

---

1. However, firms in Canada, Venezuela, Spain, and other countries that feel no commitment to U.S. global imperialism have been trading with Cuba, much to Washington's displeasure. U.S. law prevents foreign vessels that trade with Cuba from loading or unloading in the USA for six months, thus inflicting a substantial cost on Cuba and any trading partner.

Council, and the CIA. These agencies conjure up new enemies and crises because they need to justify their own existence and augment their budget allocations. This view avoids the realities of class interest and power. It suggests that policymakers serve no purpose other than policymaking for their own bureaucratic aggrandizement. Such a notion reverses cause and effect. It is a little like saying the horse is the cause of the horse race. It treats the national security state as the originator of intervention, when in fact it is but one of the major instruments. U.S. leaders were engaging in interventionist actions long before the CIA and NSC existed.

One of those who argues that the state is a self-generated aggrandizer is Richard Barnet, who dismisses the "more familiar and more sinister motives" of economic imperialism. Whatever their economic systems, all large industrial states, he maintains, seek to project power and influence in a search for security and domination. To be sure, the search for security is a real consideration for every state. But the captial investments of multinational corporations expand in a far more dynamic way than the economic expansion manifested by socialist or precapitalist governments.

In fact, the case studies in Barnet's book *Intervention and Revolution* point to business, rather than the national security bureaucracies, as the primary motive of U.S. intervention. Anticommunism and the Soviet threat seem less a source for policy than a propaganda ploy to frighten the American public and rally support for overseas commitments. The very motives Barnet dismisses seem to be operative in his case studies of Greece, Iran, Lebanon, and the Dominican Republic, specifically the desire to secure access to markets and raw materials and the need, explicitly stated by various policymakers, to protect free enterprise throughout the world.

Some might complain that the foregoing analysis is "simplistic" because it ascribes all international events to purely economic and class motives and ignores other variables like geopolitics, culture, ethnicity, nationalism, ideology, and morality. But I do not argue that the struggle to maintain capitalist global hegemony explains everything about world politics nor even everything about U.S. foreign policy. However, it explains quite a lot; so is it not time we become aware of it? If mainstream opinion makers really want to portray political life in all its manifold complexities, then why are they so studiously reticent about the immense realities of imperialism?

The existence of other variables such as nationalism, militarism, the search for national security, and the pursuit of power and hegemonic dominance, neither compels us to dismiss economic realities, nor to treat these other variables as insulated from class interests. Thus the desire to extend U.S. strategic power into a particular region is impelled at least in part by a desire to stabilize the area along lines that are favorable to politico-economic elite interests—which is why the region becomes a focus of concern in the first place.

In other words, various considerations work with circular effect upon one another. The growth in overseas investments invite a need for military protection. This, in turn, creates a need to secure bases and establish alliances with other nations. The alliances now expand the "defense" perimeter that must be maintained. So a particular country becomes not only an "essential" asset for our defense but must itself be defended, like any other asset.

Inventing Enemies

As noted in the previous chapter, the U.S. empire is neoimperialist in its operational mode. With the exception of a few territorial possessions, its overseas expansion has relied on indirect control rather than direct possession. This is not to say that U.S. leaders are strangers to annexation and conquest. Most of what is now the continental United States was forcibly wrested from Native American nations. California and all of the Southwest USA were taken from Mexico by war. Florida and Puerto Rico were seized from Spain.

U.S. leaders must convince the American people that the immense costs of empire are necessary for their security and survival. For years we were told that the great danger we faced was "the World Communist Menace with its headquarters in Moscow." The public accepted a crushing tax burden to win the superpower arms race and "contain Soviet aggression wherever it might arise." Since the demise of the USSR, our political leaders have been warning us that the world is full of other dangerous adversaries, who apparently had been previously overlooked.

Who are these evil adversaries who wait to spring upon the USA the moment we drop our guard or the moment we make real cuts in our gargantuan military budget? Why do they stalk us instead of, say, Denmark or Brazil? This scenario of a world of enemies was used by the rulers of the Roman Empire and by nineteenth-century British imperialists. Enemies always had to be confronted, requiring more interventions and more expansion. And if enemies were not to be found, they were invented.

When Washington says "our" interests must be protected abroad, we might question whether all of us are represented by the goals pursued. Far-off countries, previously unknown to most Americans, suddenly become vital to "our" interests. To protect "our" oil in the Middle East and "our" resources and "our" markets elsewhere, *our* sons and daughters have to participate in overseas military ventures, and *our* taxes are needed to finance these ventures.

The next time "our" oil in the Middle East is in jeopardy, we might remember that relatively few of us own oil stock. Yet even portfolio-deprived Americans are presumed to have a common interest with Exxon and Mobil because they live in an economy dependent on oil. It is assumed that if the people of other lands wrested control of their oil away from the big U.S. companies, they would refuse to sell it to us. Supposedly they would prefer to drive us into the arms of competing producers and themselves into ruination, denying themselves the billions of dollars they might earn on the North American market.

In fact, nations that acquire control of their own resources do not act so strangely. Cuba, Vietnam, North Korea, Libya, and others would be happy to have access to markets in this country, selling at prices equal to or lower than those offered by the giant multinationals. So when Third World peoples, through nationalization, revolution, or both, reclaim the oil in their own land, or the copper, tin, sugar, or other resources, it does not hurt the interests of the U.S. working populace. But it certainly hurts the multinational conglomerates that once profited so handsomely from these enterprises.

Who Pays? Who Profits?

We are made to believe that the people of the United States have a common interest with the giant multinationals, the very companies that desert our communities in pursuit of cheaper labor abroad. In truth, on almost every issue the people are not in the same boat with the big companies. Policy costs are not equally shared; benefits are not equally enjoyed. The "national" policies of an imperialist country reflect the interests of that country's dominant socio-economic class. Class rather than nation-state more often is the crucial unit of analysis in the study of imperialism.

The tendency to deny the existence of conflicting class interests when dealing with imperialism leads to some serious misunderstandings. For example, liberal writers like Kenneth Boulding and Richard Barnet have pointed out that empires cost more than they bring in, especially when wars are fought to maintain them. Thus, from 1950 to 1970, the U.S. government spent several billions of dollars to shore up a corrupt dictatorship in the Philippines, hoping to protect about $1 billion in U.S. investments in that country. At first glance it does not make sense to spend $3 billion to protect $1 billion. Saul Landau has made this same point in regard to the costs of U.S. interventions in Central America: they exceed actual U.S. investments. Barnet notes that "the costs of maintaining imperial privilege always exceed the gains." From this it has been concluded that empires simply are not worth all the expense and trouble. Long before Barnet, the Round Table imperialist policymakers in Great Britain wanted us to believe that the empire was not maintained because of profit; indeed "from a purely material point of view the Empire is a burden rather than a source of gain" (*Round Table*, vol. 1, 232–39, 411).

To be sure, empires do not come cheap. Burdensome expenditures are needed for military repression and prolonged occupation, for colonial administration, for bribes and arms to native collaborators, and for the development of a commercial infrastructure to facilitate extractive industries and capital penetration. But empires are not losing propositions for everyone. The governments of imperial nations may spend more than they take in, but the people who reap the benefits are not the same ones who foot the bill. As Thorstein Veblen pointed out in *The Theory of the Business Enterprise* (1904), the gains of empire flow into the hands of the privileged business class while the costs are extracted from "the industry of the rest of the people." The transnationals monopolize the private returns of empire while carrying little, if any, of the public cost. The expenditures needed in the way of armaments and aid to make the world safe for General Motors, General Dynamics, General Electric, and all the other generals are paid by the U.S. government, that is, by the taxpayers.

So it was with the British Empire in India, the costs of which, Marx noted a half-century before Veblen, were "paid out of the pockets of the people of England," and far exceeded what came back into the British treasury. He concluded that the advantage to Great Britain from her Indian Empire was limited to the "very considerable" profits which accrued to select individuals, mostly a coterie of stockholders and officers in the East India Company and the Bank of England.

Beginning in the late nineteenth century and carrying over into the twentieth, the German conquest of Southwest Africa "remained a loss-making enterprise for the German taxpayer," according to historian Horst Drechsler, yet "a number of monopolists still managed to squeeze huge profits out of the colony in the closing years of German colonial domination." And imperialism remains today in the service of the few monopolists, not the many taxpayers.

In sum, there is nothing irrational about spending three dollars of public money to protect one dollar of private investment—at least not from the perspective of the investors. To protect one dollar of their money they will spend three, four, and five dollars of our money. In fact, when it comes to protecting their money, our money is no object.

Furthermore, the cost of a particular U.S. intervention must be measured not against the value of U.S. investments in the country involved but against the value of the world investment system. It has been noted that the cost of apprehending a bank robber may occasionally exceed the sum that is stolen. But if robbers were allowed to go their way, this would encourage others to follow suit and would put the entire banking system in jeopardy.

At stake in these various wars of suppression, then, is not just the investments in any one country but the security of the whole international system of finance capital. No country is allowed to pursue an independent course of self-development. None is permitted to go unpunished and undeterred. None should serve as an inspiration or source of material support to other nations that might want to pursue a politico-economic path other than the maldevelopment offered by global capitalism.

The Myth of Popular Imperialism

Those who think of empire solely as an expression of national interests rather than class interests are bound to misinterpret the nature of imperialism. In his *American Diplomacy 1900–1950*, George Kennan describes U.S. imperialist expansion at the end of the nineteenth century as a product of popular aspiration: the American people "simply liked the smell of empire"; they wanted "to bask in the sunshine of recognition as one of the great imperial powers of the world."

In the *Progressive* (October 1984), the liberal writers John Buell and Matthew Rothschild comment that "the American psyche is pegged to being biggest, best, richest, and strongest. Just listen to the rhetoric of our politicians." But does the politician's rhetoric really reflect the sentiments of most Americans, who in fact come up decidedly noninterventionist in most opinion polls? Buell and Rothschild assert that "when a Third World nation—whether it be Cuba, Vietnam, Iran, or Nicaragua—spurns our way of doing things, our egos ache . . ." Actually, such countries spurn the ways of global corporate capitalism—and this is what U.S. politico-economic leaders will not tolerate. Psychologizing about aching collective egos allows us to blame imperialism on ordinary U.S. citizens who are neither the creators nor beneficiaries of empire.

In like fashion, the historian William Appleman Williams, in his *Empire As a Way of Life*, scolds the American people for having become addicted to the conditions of empire. It seems "we" like empire. "We" live beyond our means and need empire as part of our way of life. "We" exploit the rest of the world and don't know how to get back to a simpler life. The implication is that "we" are profiting from the runaway firms that are exporting our jobs and exploiting Third World peoples. "We" decided to send troops into Central America, Vietnam, and the Middle East and thought to overthrow democratic governments in a dozen or more countries around the world. And "we" urged the building of a global network of counterinsurgency, police torturers, and death squads in numerous countries.

For Williams, imperialist policy is a product of mass thinking. In truth, ordinary Americans usually have opposed intervention or given only lukewarm support. Opinion polls during the Vietnam War showed that the public wanted a negotiated settlement and withdrawal of U.S. troops. The American people supported the idea of a coalition government in Vietnam that included the communists, and they supported elections even if the communists won them.

Pollster Louis Harris reported that, during 1982–84 Americans rejected increased military aid for El Salvador and its autocratic military machine by more than 3 to 1. Network surveys found that 80 percent opposed sending troops to that country; 67 percent were against the U.S. mining of Nicaragua's harbors; and 2 to 1 majorities opposed aid to the Nicaraguan Contras (the right-wing CIA-supported mercenary army that was waging a brutal war of attrition against Nicaraguan civilians). A 1983 *Washington Post*/ABC News poll found that, by a 6 to 1 ratio, our citizens opposed any attempt by the United States to overthrow the Nicaraguan government. By more than 2 to 1 the public said the greatest cause of unrest in Central America was not subversion from Cuba, Nicaragua, or the Soviet Union but "poverty and the lack of human rights in the area."

Even the public's superpatriotic yellow-ribbon binge during the more recent Gulf War of 1991 was not the cause of the war itself. It was only one of the disgusting and disheartening by-products. Up to the eve of that conflict, opinion polls showed Americans favoring a negotiated withdrawal of Iraqi troops rather than direct U.S. military engagement. But once U.S. forces were committed to action, then the "support-our-troops" and "go for victory" mentality took hold of the public, pumped up as always by a jingoistic media propaganda machine.

Once war comes, especially with the promise of a quick and easy victory, some individuals suspend all critical judgment and respond on cue like mindless superpatriots. One can point to the small businessman in Massachusetts, who announced that he was a "strong supporter" of the U.S. military involvement in the Gulf, yet admitted he was not sure what the war was about. "That's something I would like to know," he stated. "What are we fighting about?" (*New York Times*, November 15, 1990).

In the afterglow of the Gulf triumph, George Bush had a 93 percent approval rating and was deemed unbeatable for reelection in 1992. Yet within a year, Americans had come down from their yellow-ribbon binge and experienced a postbellum depression, filled with worries about jobs, money, taxes, and other such realities. Bush's popularity all but evaporated and he was defeated by a scandal-plagued, relatively unknown governor from Arkansas.

Whether they support or oppose a particular intervention, the American people cannot be considered the motivating force of the war policy. They do not sweep their leaders into war on a tide of popular hysteria. It is the other way around. Their leaders take *them* for a ride and bring out the worst in them. Even then, there are hundreds of thousands who remain actively opposed and millions who correctly suspect that such ventures are not in their interest.

Cultural Imperialism

Imperialism exercises control over the communication universe. American movies, television shows, music, fashions, and consumer products inundate Latin America, Asia, and Africa, as well as Western and Eastern Europe. U.S. rock stars and other performers play before wildly enthusiastic audiences from Madrid to Moscow, from Rio to Bangkok. U.S. advertising agencies dominate the publicity and advertising industries of the world.

Millions of news reports, photographs, commentaries, editorials, syndicated columns, and feature stories from U.S. media saturate most other countries each year. Millions of comic books and magazines, condemning communism and boosting the wonders of the free market, are translated into dozens of languages and distributed by U.S. (dis)information agencies. The CIA alone owns outright over 200 newspapers, magazines, wire services, and publishing houses in countries throughout the world.

U.S. government–funded agencies like the National Endowment for Democracy and the Agency for International Development, along with the Ford Foundation and other such organizations, help maintain Third World universities, providing money for academic programs, social science institutes, research, student scholarships, and textbooks supportive of a free market ideological perspective. Right-wing Christian missionary agencies preach political quiescence and anticommunism to native populations. The AFL-CIO's American Institute for Free Labor Development (AIFLD), with ample State Department funding, has actively infiltrated Third World labor organizations or built compliant unions that are more anticommunist than proworker. AIFLD graduates have been linked to coups and counterinsurgency work in various countries. Similar AFL-CIO undertakings operate in Africa and Asia.

The CIA has infiltrated important political organizations in numerous countries and maintains agents at the highest levels of various governments, including heads of state, military leaders, and major political parties. Washington has financed conservative political parties in Latin America, Asia, Africa, and Western and Eastern Europe. Their major qualification is that they be friendly to Western capital penetration. While federal law prohibits foreigners from making campaign contributions to U.S. candidates, Washington policymakers reserve the right to interfere in the elections of other countries, such as Italy, the Dominican Republic, Panama, Nicaragua, and El Salvador, to name only a few. U.S. leaders feel free to intrude massively upon the economic, military, political, and cultural practices and institutions of any country they so choose. That's what it means to have an empire.

CHAPTER 4

STRONG EMPIRE, WEAK REPUBLIC

The success of the empire depends upon its ability to expropriate the resources of the republic. In the previous chapter we noted how the financial burdens of imperialism are sustained by the ordinary taxpayers, while the benefits accrue to the favored few. There are additional ways that Americans pay the hidden costs of empire.

Exporting Jobs

As early as 1916, Lenin pointed out that as it advanced, capitalism would export not only its goods but its very capital, not only its products but its entire production process. Today, most giant U.S. firms do just that, exporting their technology, factories, and sales networks—and our jobs. It is well known that General Motors has been closing down factories in the USA. Less well known is that for many years GM has been spending millions of dollars abroad on new auto plants in countries where wages are far less than what American auto workers are paid. This means bigger profits for GM and more unemployment for Detroit.

Over the last twenty years, American firms have tripled their total outlay in other countries, their fastest growth rate being in the Third World. Nor is the trend likely to reverse itself. American capitalism is now producing abroad eight times more than it exports. Many firms have shifted all their manufacturing activities to foreign lands. All the cameras sold in the USA are made overseas, as are almost all the bicycles, tape recorders, radios, television sets, VCRs, and computers. One of every three workers now employed by U.S. multinational companies works in a foreign country. U.S. companies continue to export tens of thousands of stateside jobs each year. Management's threat to relocate a plant is often sufficient to black-mail U.S. workers into taking wage and benefit cuts and working longer hours.

We are victimized by economic imperialism not only as workers but as taxpayers and consumers. Multinationals do not have to pay U.S. taxes on profits made in other countries until these profits are repatriated to the USA—if ever they are. Taxes paid to a host coun-try are treated as tax credits rather than mere deductions here at home. In other words, $1 million paid to a foreign country in taxes or even oil royalties is not treated as a deduction of taxable income by the IRS (which might save the company $100,000 or so in state-side taxes), but is written off from the final taxes the company has to pay, saving it an entire $1 million in payments.

In addition, multinationals can juggle the books between their various foreign subsidiaries, showing low profits in a high-tax coun-try and high profits in a low-tax country, thereby avoiding at least $20 billion a year in U.S. taxes.

The billions that corporations escape paying because of their overseas shelters must be made up by the rest of us. Additional bil-lions of our tax dollars go into aid programs to governments that maintain the cheap labor markets that lure away American jobs. U.S.

foreign aid seldom trickles down to the poor people of the recipient countries. In fact, much of it is military aid that is likely to be used to suppress dissent among the poor. Our tax money also is used to finance the construction of roads, office complexes, plants, and ports needed to support extractive industries in the Third World.

Nor do the benefits of this empire trickle down to the American consumer in any appreciable way. Generally the goods made abroad by superexploited labor are sold at as high a price as possible on U.S. markets. Corporations move to Asia and Africa not to produce lower-priced goods that will save money for U.S. consumers but to maximize their profits. They pay as little as possible in wages abroad but still charge as much as possible when they sell the goods at home. Shoes that cost Nike $7 to make in Indonesia—where the company or its subcontractors pay women workers about 18 cents an hour—are then sold in this country for $130 or more. Baseballs produced in Haiti at a labor cost of two cents a ball are sold in the USA for $10 and up. The General Electric household appliances made by young women in South Korea, who work for bare subsistence wages, and the Admiral International color television sets assembled by low-paid workers in Taiwan, do not cost us any less than when they were made in North America. As the president of Admiral noted, the shift to Taiwan "won't affect pricing state-side but it should improve the company's profit structure, otherwise we wouldn't be making the move."

Nor do these overseas investments bring any great benefits to the peoples of the Third World. Foreign investment created the "Brazil Miracle," a dramatic growth in that country's gross national product in the 1960s. At the same time it created a food shortage and increased poverty, as Brazil's land and labor were used increasingly for production of cash export crops, and less for the needs of the Brazilian people. In Central America, land that once yielded corn and beans to feed the people has been converted to cattle ranches that raise the beef consumed in North America and Europe.

We have heard much about the "refugees from communism"; we might think a moment about the refugees from capitalism. Driven off their lands, large numbers of impoverished Latinos and other Third Worlders have been compelled to flee into economic exile, coming to the United States, many of them illegally, to compete with U.S. workers for entry-level jobs. Because of their illegal status and vulnerability to deportation, undocumented workers are least likely to unionize and least able to fight for improvements in work conditions.

Empire Against Environment

For years the herbicides, pesticides, and hazardous pharmaceuticals that were banned in this country have been sold by their producers to Third World nations where regulations are weaker or nonexistent. (In 1981, President Reagan repealed an executive order signed by President Carter that would have forced exporters of such products to notify the recipient nation that the commodity was banned in the USA.) With an assured export market, these poisons continue to cripple workers in the American chemical plants where they are made, and then reappear on our dinner tables in the fruit, vegetables, meat, and coffee we import. Such products also have been poisoning people in Third World countries, creating a legacy of sickness and death.

With the passage of GATT, it will be easier than ever to bypass consumer and environmental protections. The chemical toxins and other industrial effusions poured into the world's groundwater, oceans, and atmosphere by fast-profit, unrestricted multinational corporations operating in Asia, Africa, and Latin America, and the devastation of Third World lands by mining and timber companies and agribusiness, are seriously affecting the quality of the air we breathe, the water we drink, and the food we eat. Ecology knows no national boundaries.

The search for cheap farmland to raise cattle induces companies to cut down rain forests throughout Central America, South America, and Southeast Asia. This depletion of the global ecological base is a threat to all the earth's inhabitants. The tropical rain forests in Central America and the larger ones in the Amazon basin may be totally obliterated within the next two decades. Over 25 percent of our prescription drugs are derived from rain forest plants. Rain forests are the winter home for millions of migratory North American songbirds—of which declining numbers are returning from Central America. Many of these birds are essential to pest and rodent control.

Over half the world's forests are gone compared to earlier centuries. The forests are nature's main means of removing carbon dioxide from the atmosphere. Today, the carbon dioxide buildup is transforming the chemical composition of the earth's atmosphere, accelerating the "greenhouse effect," melting the earth's polar ice caps, and causing a variety of other climatic destabilizations. The dumping of industrial effusions and radioactive wastes also may be killing our oceans. If the oceans die, so do we, since they produce most of the earth's oxygen. While the imperialists are free to roam the world and defile it at will, we are left to suffer the potentially irreversible consequences.

Additional damage to the environment and wildlife is inflicted by the U.S. armed forces, which use millions of acres of land at home and abroad in bombing runs and maneuvers. For decades, over one hundred nuclear weapons plants have been pouring radioactive waste into the air, soil, groundwater, and rivers. The military is the single biggest consumer of fuel in this country and the greatest polluter, contaminating the environment with hundreds of thousands of tons of heavy metals, solvents, lubricants, PCBs, plutonium, tritium, fuel runoffs, and other toxic wastes.

The military creates over 90 percent of our radioactive waste and stockpiles thousands of tons of lethal biochemical agents. There are some 21,000 contaminated sites on military bases and at nuclear weapons plants. Each year, the military utilizes millions of tons of ozone-depleting chemicals.

In sum, one of the greatest dangers to the security and well-being of the American public and to the planet itself is the U.S. military.

American Casualties

The military is also a danger to its own ranks. Enlisted personnel are regularly killed in vehicular accidents, firing exercises, flight crashes, ship fires, and parachute jumps—resulting in 20,269 *non-combat* deaths from 1979 to 1988, or an average of 2,027 a year. In addition are the several hundred suicides that occur yearly in the armed services.

Thousands of Army veterans exposed to nuclear tests after World War II have suffered premature deaths from cancer. Vietnam veterans who came back contaminated by the tons of herbicides sprayed on Indochina are facing terminal ailments, while their children have suffered an abnormally high rate of birth defects (in common with children in Vietnam, though the latter have endured a much higher rate of abnormalities). Similarly, tens of thousands of veterans from the Gulf War of 1991 have succumbed to a variety of illnesses due to exposure to a range of war-related, lethal substances. And for many years, workers in nuclear plants and "downwinders" in Utah who were afflicted with radiation poisoning from the Nevada atomic tests have died prematurely. Many have given birth to genetically deficient children.

The U.S. military has performed chemical and bacteriological experiments on Americans. The Navy sprayed bacteria in San Francisco in 1950, an escapade that has since been implicated in the serious illness of several residents and the death of at least one person. In 1955, the CIA conducted a biological warfare test in the Tampa Bay area, soon after which twelve people died in a whooping cough epidemic. Throughout the 1950s and 1960s, there were purposeful releases of radiation from the nuclear weapons manufacturing facility at Hanford, Washington, with subsequent secret medical monitoring of the local downwind population.

In 1994 it was revealed that in the late 1940s government scientists injected perhaps hundreds of Americans with plutonium without their knowledge and for the next twenty years sprayed infectious bacilli and chemical particles in about 270 populated locations, including St. Louis, New York, and Minneapolis.

The empire strikes back home with the narcotics that are shipped into the USA through secret international cartels linked to the CIA. Large-scale drug trafficking has been associated with CIA-supported covert wars in Southeast Asia and Central America. As of 1988, evidence was mounting linking the U.S.-backed Nicaraguan Contras to a network of narcotics smuggling that stretched from cocaine plantations in Colombia to airstrips in Costa Rica, to dummy business firms in Miami—and inevitably to the drug-ridden streets of our society. As the Kerry Senate subcommittee documented, the drug epidemic of the 1980s was a direct result of this CIA-supported traffic.

The empire has a great many overhead costs, especially military ones, that must be picked up by our people. The Vietnam War's total expenditures (including veterans' benefits and hospitals, interest on the national debt, and the like) comes to well over $518 billion, as estimated by economist Victor Perlo. He pointed out that by the war's end inflation had escalated from about 1 percent a year to 10 percent; the national debt had doubled over the 1964 level; the federal budget showed record deficits; unemployment had doubled; real wages had started on their longest decline in modern U.S. history; interest rates rose to 10 percent and higher; the U.S. export surplus gave way to an import surplus; and U.S. gold and monetary reserves were drained.

There were serious human costs as well. Some 2.5 million Americans had their lives interrupted to serve in Indochina. Of these, 58,156 were killed and 303,616 wounded (13,167 with 100 percent disability). More than 70,000 have died since returning home because of suicides, murders, addictions, and alcoholism. Tens of thousands more have attempted suicide. Ethnic minorities paid a disproportionate price. While composing about 12 percent of our population, African Americans accounted for 22 percent of all combat deaths in Vietnam. The New Mexico state legislature noted that Mexican Americans constituted only 29 percent of that state's population but 69 percent of the state's inductees and 43 percent of its Vietnam casualties in the early years of the war.

Impoverishing the Republic

The empire increasingly impoverishes the republic. Operational costs of global militarism may become so onerous as to undermine the society that sustains them, such as has been the case with empires in the past. Americans pay dearly for "our" global military apparatus. The spending binge that the Pentagon has been on for decades, especially the last fourteen years or so, has created record deficits and a runaway national debt, making the United States the largest debtor nation in the world. The government is required to borrow more and more to pay the growing interest on a debt that is owed to rich creditors at home and abroad.

Between 1948 and 1994, the federal government spent almost $11 trillion on its military—more than the cumulative monetary value of all human-made wealth in the United States. The current Pentagon budget plus the military projects of the Energy Department and NASA, foreign military aid, veterans' benefits, and interest paid on past military debt comes to almost $500 billion a year. The annual Pentagon budget is more than the gross national product of almost every country in the world. Over the last decade, the average contribution per family to military spending was $35,000.

U.S. military spending is of a magnitude unmatched by any other power. In 1993, according to the Center for Defense Information, the United States spent $291 billion on the military, while second-place Japan spent $40 billion, followed by France's $36 billion, the United Kingdom's $35 billion, Germany's $31 billion, Russia's $29 billion, and China's $22 billion. In any one year, the United States spends more on the military than the next fifteen nations combined.

Most of our domestic financial woes can be ascribed to military spending. The enormous scale of that spending is sometimes hard to grasp. The cost of building one aircraft carrier could feed several million of the poorest, hungriest children in America for ten years. Greater sums have been budgeted for the development of the Navy's submarine rescue vehicle than for occupational safety, public libraries, and daycare centers combined. The cost of military aircraft components and ammunition kept in storage by the Pentagon is greater than the combined federal spending on pollution control, conservation, community development, housing, occupational safety, and mass transportation. The total expenses of the legislative and judicial branches and all the regulatory commissions combined constitute less than 1 percent of the Pentagon's yearly budget.

Then there is the distortion of U.S. science and technology, as 70 percent of federal research and development (R&D) funds goes to the military. Contrary to Pentagon claims, what the military produces in R&D has little spin-off for the civilian market. About-one third of all American scientists and engineers are involved in military projects, creating a serious brain drain for the civilian sector. The United States is losing out to foreign competitors in precisely those industries with a high military rather than civilian investment. For instance, the U.S. machine tool industry, which once dominated the world market, has seen a sixfold increase in foreign imports. The same pattern has been evident in the aerospace and electronics industries, and other areas of concentrated military investment.

Because of the disproportionate amount spent on the military, Americans must endure the neglect of environmental needs, the financial insolvency and decay of our cities, the deterioration of our transportation, education, and health care systems, and the devastating effects of underemployment upon millions of households and hundreds of communities. In addition, there are the frightful social and psychological costs, the discouragement and decline of public morale, the anger and suffering of the poor and the not-so-poor, the militarization and violence of popular culture, and the application of increasingly authoritarian solutions to our social ills.

Poverty can be found in the rich industrial nations as well as in the Third World. In the richest of them all, the United States, the number of people below the poverty level grew in the last dozen years from twenty-four million to almost thirty-five million, according to the government's own figures, which many consider to be underestimations, thus making the poor the fastest growing social group in the USA, rivaled only by the dramatic growth of millionaires and billionaires.

In recent years, tuberculosis—a disease of poverty—has made a big comeback. The House Select Committee on Hunger found that kwashiorkor and marasmus diseases, caused by severe protein and calorie deficiencies and usually seen only in Third World countries, could now be found in the United States, along with a rise in infant mortality in poor areas.

Those regions within the United States that serve as surplus labor reserves or "internal colonies," such as Appalachia, poor Latino and African American communities, Inuit Alaska, and Native-American Indian communities, manifest the symptoms of Third World colonization, including chronic underemployment, hunger, inadequate income, low levels of education, inferior or nonexistent human services, absentee ownership, and extraction of profits from the indigenous community. In addition, the loss of skilled, good-paying manufacturing jobs, traditionally held by white males, has taken a toll of working-class white communities as well.

So when we talk of "rich nations" and "poor nations" we must not forget that there are millions of poor in the rich nations and thousands of rich in the poor ones. As goes the verse by Bertolt Brecht:

> There were conquerors and conquered.
> Among the conquered the common people starved.
> Among the conquerors the common people starved too.

As in Rome of old and in every empire since, the center is bled in order to fortify the periphery. The lives and treasure of the people are squandered so that patricians might pursue their far-off plunder.

The Few Against the Many

The empire concentrates power in the hands of a few and robs the populace of effective self-rule. As James Madison wrote to Thomas Jefferson in 1798: "Perhaps it is a universal truth that the loss of liberty at home is to be charged to provisions against danger, real or pretended, from abroad."

One might respond that we should not worry too much about this, for public policy is not formulated by the people, those masses beloved and idealized by people on the Left. Average people have a low level of information by any objective measure. They seldom know what is really going on. Government policy, both domestic and foreign, almost always has its origin in the highest circles of government and within bodies such as the Council on Foreign Relations, the Trilateral Commission, and other public and private elite groups populated by top policy specialists, bankers, CEOs, investors, leading publicists, and a sprinkling of academic researchers. They are the people who inhabit the upper circles of power, who become the secretaries of state, defense, treasury, commerce, and the heads of the CIA and the National Security Council. They create and monopolize policy. The most we can expect from the public, the argument continues, is that at election time it gives its stamp of approval to one or another elite coterie of policymakers.

In response, I would agree that elites try their best to monopolize policy and mislead the public, and too often they are successful. Yet it should be pointed out that almost all policy that is worthwhile, life-affirming, and democratic in its substantive output, has come from the people. Consider the struggle for women's rights extending over the last one hundred years. What presidents, cabinet members, or high-powered policy specialists led the way in that battle? At best, some leaders belatedly took up the causes of female suffrage, affirmative action, and legal abortion only after women long agitated for such rights. So with the struggle for civil rights. Political elites reluctantly came out for a Fair Employment Practice Commission in the late 1940s, the abolition of Jim Crow in the South, a Civil Rights Voting Act in the 1960s, and other such moves only after decades of struggle by ordinary people, most of them African Americans.

It would also be hard to name the political leaders and captains of industry who fought for and not against the ten-hour day or, later on, the eight-hour day. And which of them were moving lights in the struggles for collective bargaining, public education, community health standards, and the abolition of child labor? To be sure, there were individuals from privileged backgrounds who advocated these things—but usually as individuals, not as representatives of any corporate interest or elite policy group. If these were things that the rich and the powerful had wanted, it would not have been necessary to wage such prolonged struggles to attain them.

One would be hard pressed to name the major political leaders who originated the environmental movement. Only in response to public pressures did our political leaders establish an Environmental Protection Agency, which to this day needs to be pressured by private citizens to do the things it should be doing anyway. Corporate leaders still treat environmental laws as unnecessary bureaucratic intrusions upon their pursuit of profit. Vice President Al Gore wrote an environmentalist book about the fate of the planet before taking office, then fought for NAFTA and GATT, measures designed to cripple the ability of governments to maintain environmental protections.

The consumer protection movement was started by consumers and independent investigators like Ralph Nader. Getting unsafe products off the market is not something a capitalist government does as a matter of course. Quite the contrary, the natural function of a capitalist government is to get things *onto* the market (including lethal tobacco products), using subsidies, export supports, grants-in-kind, tax breaks, free research and development, and various other forms of corporate welfarism.

So with the antinuclear movement. Far from protecting us from the dangers of fallout and radioactive wastes, the government has been busy all these years covering up and denying the unsafe features of atomic tests that led to the deaths of hundreds of U.S. soldiers and civilians.

Every day government releases a flood of publications, press releases, and deliberate leaks designed to get us to view the world the way policymakers want us to. The Pentagon has a massive propaganda machine churning out self-serving disinformation, mostly fed through the corporate-owned mainstream media. But regarding things that government does not want us to know, secrecy is the rule. What political leader originated the idea of a Freedom of Information Act? Such legislation was enacted only after much organized effort by nongovernmental critics.

Government classifies millions of documents each year, often for fifty years or more, inking out large portions of them, shredding many others and thereby distorting history, keeping critical independent researchers from the entire story. One has the distinct impression that the job of policy officials is to undermine the Freedom of Information Act, while the public's job is to fight for information, something that would not be necessary if politico-economic elites had nothing to hide and were really interested in serving the public interest.

This is not to say that no policies originate with the power-wielders. They originated the Manhattan Project to build an atomic bomb. They developed the nuclear industry, then handed it over to private business at a fraction of its original cost, subsidized yearly with vast sums from the public treasury. They created the FBI, the CIA, the entire national security state apparatus, and the U.S. global military network. They gave us McCarthyism, political witch hunts, loyalty and security programs to purge dissenters from government, the secret surveillance of our personal lives, and the push for ideological orthodoxy.

There are other elite policy creations: the foreign aid programs to military dictators and the setting up of security forces, death squads, and torturers, with all the necessary funding and technology. Nor should we forget the bombers and missiles, and the costly interventions in scores of countries. Generally speaking, policy elites serve the needs of state domination and manipulation, and are resistant to the life-affirming policies for which we have to struggle so long and hard.

A Moral Self-Interest

If we are to mobilize resistance to the empire, we must appeal not only to people's moral values but to their self-interest (and I do not mean their selfishness). People may rally around the banners of empire when convinced that their security and survival are at stake. They will not choose morality if they think it brings endangerment to them and their loved ones. Nor will they choose disarmament and peaceful conversion if they think it will show weakness and invite aggression against themselves.

So they must be shown that the republic is being bled for the empire's profits, not for their well-being, that real national security means secure jobs, safe homes, and a clean environment. They must be informed that this empire, which is paid for by their blood, sweat, and taxes, has little to do with protecting them or people abroad and everything to do with victimizing them in order to feed the power and profits of the few. The global military apparatus they grudgingly support at such immense costs does not serve their interests. To cut it drastically will not leave us prey to some foreign adversaries. On the contrary, to lay down the sword and use our labor and national treasure for the peaceful reconstruction so desperately needed at home and abroad is not to become a weak nation but a truly great one.

Mainstream pundits and propagandists label our desire to move away from corporate militarism and imperial domination as weakness, folly, isolationism, or self-defeating pacifism. But there is another name for the course of action that aims to wrest the wealth and power out of the hands of the military-industrial complex and the multinational investor class and give it back to the people so that they become the agents of their own lives and social conditions: it is called democracy, the victory of the republic over the empire.

These same propagandists dismiss criticisms of U.S. imperialism as manifestations of a "Hate America" or "Blame America" syndrome. But when we voice our disapproval of militarism, violent interventions, and other particular policies, we are not attacking our nation and its people; rather we are maintaining that we deserve something better than the policies that currently violate the interests of people at home and abroad. To expose the abuses of class power is not to denigrate the nation that is a victim of such abuses.

With more justification, we might conclude that it is the conservatives who lack patriotism when they denounce spending on human services, environmental protections, and more equitable taxes. The charge of anti-Americanism is selectively and self-servingly applied, against those on the Left who struggle for the interests of the many, rather than against those on the Right who serve the interests of the few. Those who oppose empire are thought to be against the republic, when actually they are its last best hope.

CHAPTER 5

A DREADFUL SUCCESS

There are those who criticize U.S. foreign policy for its blunders and lack of coherence. To be sure, policymakers miscalculate. At times they are taken by surprise, frustrated by unintended consequences, or thwarted by forces beyond their control. They are neither infallible nor omnipotent. But neither are they the blind fools that some people think them to be. Overall, U.S. foreign policy has been remarkably successful in undermining popular revolutions and buttressing conservative capitalist regimes in every region of the world. Were it not for such successes, the history of Latin America, the Caribbean, Asia, Africa, the Middle East, and postwar Europe itself would have taken a dramatically different course.

Many Americans recognize that politicians lie, that they are capable of saying one thing then doing another, that they loudly proclaim a dedication to the people while quietly serving powerful interests. But when it comes to U.S. foreign policy, many of us retreat from that judgment. Suddenly we find it hard to believe that U.S. leaders would lie to us about their intentions in the world, and that they pursue neoimperialist policies having little to do with democracy.

Unexamined Assumptions

We are told that this nation's foreign policy emanates from the best motives and adheres to lawful standards of international conduct. On the infrequent occasions that foreign policy is debated in the political mainstream and major media, criticism is limited to operational questions: Are our leaders relying too much (or too little) on military force? Are they trying to impose a Western style democracy on people who are not ready for it? Are they failing to act decisively? Have they waited too long or rushed in too hastily? Will the policy succeed? Will it prove too costly?

Rarely, if ever, are basic policy premises examined. It is accepted as a matter of course that the United States has a right to intervene in the affairs of other nations to restore order, thwart aggression, fight terrorism, rescue endangered Americans, or whatever. It is taken as given that unjust aggression is something this country resists but never practices, that conflicts arising with other nations are the fault of those nations, that leftists are dangerous but rightists usually are not, that there is no need to define what *is* a leftist or a rightist, and that something called "stability" is preferred to revolution and popular agitation.

The basic indictment of this book—that U.S. policy serves mostly the favored few rather than the common people in this country and abroad—is given no recognition in mainstream political discussion and media commentary.[1] From Argentina to Zaire, from East Timor to the Western Sahara, U.S.-sponsored counterrevolutionary cam-

---

1. For a more detailed discussion of the media's role in covering up the crimes of empire, see my *Inventing Reality, The Politics of News Media,* 2nd edition (New York: St. Martin's Press, 1993).

paigns of attrition have taken millions of lives, with tens of millions wounded, maimed, emotionally shattered, displaced, or exiled. Yet one hears hardly a word about it in what passes for political discourse in this country.

We are told that this nation is under an obligation to demonstrate its resolve, that it must constantly display its strength, flex its muscles, and act like a great superpower so as not to be pushed around by some small upstart nation (an argument used to justify the pulverization of Vietnam and the massacre in Iraq). Any failure to apply our power, we hear, undermines our credibility and invites aggression. One might wonder why U.S. leaders feel such a need to convince everyone else that the United States is the strongest military power in the world—when everyone else is already painfully aware of that fact.

Macho Posturing

Some say the need arises from a psychological insecurity that generations of U.S. leaders have suffered in common. To be sure, presidents are often given to macho posturing to convey the impression that they are decisive and forceful. The key enforcement instrument of state power, the military, is built on machismo, with all its attendant emphasis on toughness, domination, and violence. But while macho feelings and images are encouraged and harnessed, they do not of themselves explain the policies of empire.

No doubt President Bush wanted to demonstrate his toughness when he attacked Panama and Iraq, but he was impelled less by macho impulse than by political interests. He was also nursing a consuming desire to improve his approval ratings and get reelected. Likewise, President Clinton's air strike early in his presidency against Iraq was a flexing of image muscles, his presidential blooding, designed to demonstrate that he was no wimp and was capable of using lethal force when "necessary." In short, the goal is not macho indulgence per se but getting reelected. If cross-dressing in a skirt and heels would guarantee reelection, Clinton and every other male politician would throw machismo to the wind and attire themselves accordingly.

A show of force rallies the public around its leaders, for the people have been made to believe that such force is necessary for the nation's survival and their own security. Most ordinary citizens do not wish to engage in combat. They must be drafted. Even most volunteers join the army not out of a macho desire to kill and be killed but to find some economic opportunity or means of support. Rather than being impelled by their testosterone to charge into battle, most soldiers have to be ordered to do so under threat of severe sanctions.

Those who see empire as arising from the macho need to dominate do not explain why U.S. leaders want to dominate some nations rather than others. The machismo theory does not explain why Washington comes down so consistently on the side of transnational corporate interests, landowners, and military autocrats rather than on the side of workers, peasants, students, and others who struggle for egalitarian reforms.

Without too much regard for their manly images, policymakers have been most accommodating toward client-state, right-wing dictatorships. If not complete pushovers, they certainly lean over backward in a most unmacho way, sending generous aid without asking too many questions about how it is spent, and striving to stay on good terms with an unsavory assortment of juntas, autocrats, and corrupt politicians.

Often we are asked to believe that the United States not only has a right to intervene abroad but an obligation. It is said "we must accept the responsibilities thrust upon us." No hint is offered as to who has been doing the thrusting and why this country must meddle in every corner of the world. In 1992, President Bush announced that the United States was "the world leader" and that other countries expected us to act as such. Successive White House occupants, unable to clean up our waterways or develop rational energy systems or provide jobs and decent housing for millions at home, proclaim themselves leaders of the entire world.

In actual practice, being "world leader" means having primary responsibility for maintaining the global system of capital investment and accumulation. The task is to bring resistent elements to heel, using every form of control and attrition to keep various peoples within the impoverished client-state fold. They must cry "uncle," as President Reagan said he wanted revolutionary Nicaragua to do—and as indeed it did along with revolutionary Ethiopia and Mozambique after enough years of U.S.-sponsored battering.

In the Name of Democracy

One repeatedly hears that U.S. leaders oppose communist countries because they lack political democracy. But, as noted earlier, successive administrations in Washington have supported some of the most repressive regimes in the world, ones that regularly have indulged in mass arrests, assassination, torture, and intimidation. In addition, Washington has supported some of the worst right-wing counterrevolutionary rebel cutthroats: Savimbi's UNITA in Angola, RENAMO in Mozambique, the mujahideen in Afghanistan, and in the 1980s even the Pol Pot lunatics who waged war against socialist Cambodia.

Consider the case of Cuba. We are asked to believe that decades of U.S. hostility toward Cuba—including embargo, sabotage, and invasion—have been motivated by a distaste for the autocratic nature of the Castro government and a concern for the freedoms of the Cuban people. Whence this sudden urge to "restore" Cuban liberty? In the decades before the Cuban Revolution of 1959, successive U.S. administrations backed a brutally repressive autocracy headed by General Fulgencio Batista. The significant but unspoken difference was that Batista was a comprador leader who left Cuba wide open to U.S. capital penetration. In contrast, Fidel Castro did away with private corporate control of the economy, nationalized U.S. holdings, and renovated the class structure in a more collectivized and egalitarian mode. That is what made him so insufferable.

Far from supporting democracy around the world, the U.S. national security state since World War II has played an active role in the destruction of progressive democratic governments in some two dozen countries.[2] In justifying the overthrow of Chile's democratically elected president, Salvador Allende, in 1973, Henry Kissinger remarked that when we have to chose between the economy and democracy, we must save the economy. Kissinger was uttering a half-truth. It would have been the whole truth if he had said he wanted to save the *capitalist* economy.

It was not Allende who wrecked the Chilean economy. Upper-class privilege, widespread corruption, and mass poverty were securely in place generations before he took office. If anything, in two short years, his Popular Unity government brought about a noticeable shift of the gross national income, away from the wealthy elites who lived off interest, dividends, and rents, and toward those who lived off wages and salaries. In Allende's Chile there was a small but real modification of class power. The rich were rationed in consumer goods and were expected to pay taxes. Some of their holdings and businesses were nationalized. Meanwhile, the poor benefited from public works employment, literacy programs, worker cooperatives, and a free half-liter of milk each day for every poor child.

---

2. See Chapter 3 for a listing.

In addition, a few of Chile's radio and television stations began to offer a view of public affairs that departed from the ideological monopoly of the nation's privately owned media. Far from endangering democracy, the leftist Popular Unity government was endangering the privileged oligarchs—by expanding democracy.

What alarmed leaders like Kissinger was not that Allende's social democratic reforms were failing but that they were succeeding. The trend toward politico-economic equality had to be stopped. So Kissinger, the CIA, the White House, and the U.S. media went after the Popular Unity government tooth and nail. In the name of saving Chile's democracy, they destroyed it, instituting a fascist dictatorship under General Augusto Pinochet, one that tortured and executed thousands, disappeared thousands more, and suppressed all opposition media, political parties, labor unions, and peasant organizations.

Immediately after the military coup, General Motors, which had closed its plants when Allende was elected, resumed operations, demonstrating how capitalism is much more comfortable with fascism than with social democracy. Far from rescuing the economy, the CIA-sponsored coup ushered in an era of skyrocketing inflation and national debt, with drastic increases in unemployment, poverty, and hunger.

The Hunt for Red Menace

Official Washington cannot tell the American people that the real purpose of its gargantuan military expenditures and belligerent interventions is to make the world safe for General Motors, General Electric, General Dynamics, and all the other generals. Instead we are told that our nation's security is at stake. But it is not easy to convince the public that minipowers like Cuba, Panama, or Nicaragua, or a micropower like Grenada are a threat to our survival. So during the Cold War we were told that such countries were instruments of Soviet world aggrandizement.

Not long after the Cuban people overthrew the Batista dictatorship, President Eisenhower announced that Washington could not tolerate in the Western hemisphere a regime "dominated by international communism." Cuba was depicted as part of a world conspiracy with its headquarters in Moscow. For decades, "Soviet expansionism" served as the bogey that justified U.S. interventionism.

To be sure, the Soviet Union and the other Eastern European communist governments did pose a threat to global capitalism. They developed large public-sector economies and gave aid to anti-imperialist countries and movements around the world, including Nelson Mandela's African National Congress in South Africa. In addition, the Soviet Union's nuclear capability imposed an occasional brake on the scope and level of U.S. military intervention. Thus President Bush might have acted with more circumspection against Iraq in 1991 had the Soviet bloc still been in existence and in firm opposition to such action.

If the U.S. global military machine was a necessary response to Soviet aggression, as we were repeatedly asked to believe, why does it continue to exist well after the USSR and the Warsaw Pact military alliance have dissolved and the Cold War is declared to be over? As CIA director Robert Gates admitted, "The threat to the United States of deliberate attack from that quarter has all but disappeared for the foreseeable future" (*New York Times*, January 23, 1992).

Officials set about to convince us that new enemies suddenly had emerged. Defense Secretary Dick Cheney announced that the Soviet Union had not been the only threat; the world was full of other dangerous adversaries—whom he apparently had previously overlooked. We were now told that troubles could arise from within Third World countries themselves, even without any instigation from Moscow. U.S. policymakers and their dutiful mouthpieces in the corporate-owned media alerted us to the mortal peril posed by international terrorists, Islamic fanatics, narco-killer cartels, nuclear madmen, and Third World Hitlers. The few remaining communist governments such as North Korea and Cuba were no longer portrayed as instruments of Moscow but as evils in their own right.

For decades we were told that we needed an enormous navy to protect us from the USSR. With the Soviet Union no longer in existence, Admiral Trost, chief of naval operations, announced that we still needed an enormous navy because it did other things besides defend us from the Soviet Union. The navy, he said, must go to trouble spots and "show the flag"—vintage imperialist terminology for the practice of sending battleships to foreign ports to intimidate restive populations with a display of strength. The ships do not show the flag so much as they show their guns, the long-range ones that can lob death and destruction many miles inland. Such displays also have been referred to as "gunboat diplomacy." Today, it is less likely to be a gunboat or battleship than a naval task force with aircraft carriers, fighter bombers, missiles, and helicopter gunships.

Trost added that a powerful navy was needed for "local and regional conflicts." It was the self-anointed task of the United States to police a troubled world. But *cui bono*? For whose benefit and at whose expense was the policing done? Officials do not usually say that their job is to protect global capitalism from egalitarian social movements. They prefer coded terms such as "local and regional conflicts." And when all else fails, they talk about defending "our interests" abroad, a catch-all phrase that justifies almost any action.

What Are "Our Interests"?

While participating in a conference in New York, I heard Michael Harrington, the late leader of Democratic Socialists of America, speaking about U.S. foreign policy. During the question period, somebody asked him why was U.S. policy "so stupid?" Harrington replied that "we are the good Germans" and "we are the busybodies" of the world and "we have this power thing."

I responded that, rather than being stupid, U.S. policy is, for the most part, remarkably successful and brutal in the service of elite economic interests. It may seem stupid because the rationales offered in its support often sound unconvincing, leaving us with the impression that policymakers are confused or out of touch. But just because the public does not understand what they are doing does not mean national security leaders are themselves befuddled. That they are fabricators does not mean they are fools. While costly in money, lives, and human suffering, U.S. policy is essentially a rational and consistent enterprise. Certainly the pattern of who is supported and who opposed, who is treated as friend and who as foe, indicates as much.

I added that we should stop saying "we" do this and "we" do that, since we really mean policymakers within the national security establishment who represent a particular set of class interests. Too many otherwise capable analysts have this habit of referring to "we." It is a shorthand way of saying "U.S. national security state leaders" but it is a misleading use of a pronoun. The point is of more than semantic significance. Those who keep saying "we" are more likely to treat nations as the basic unit of analysis in international affairs and to ignore class interests. They are more likely to presume that a community of interest exists between leaders and populace when usually it does not. The impression left is that *we are* all responsible for "our" policy, a position that takes the heat off the actual policymakers and evokes a lot of misplaced soul-searching by well-meaning persons who conclude that we all should be shamed and saddened by what "we" are doing in the world.

All economic policy, not just its foreign policy aspects, is formulated from one or another class perspective. The economy itself is not a neutral entity. Strictly speaking, there is no such thing as "the economy." Nobody has ever seen or touched an economy. What we see are people engaged in the exchange of values, in productive and not such productive labor, and we give an overarching name to all these activities, calling them "the economy," a hypothetical construct imposed on observable actualities. We then often treat our abstractions as reified entities, as self-generating forces of their own. So we talk about the problems of the economy in general terms, not the problems of the *capitalist* economy with a specific set of social relations and a discernible distribution of class power. The economy becomes an embodied entity unto itself, as in statements like, "The economy is in a slump" and "the economy is reviving."

In the same way, we abstract then reify the concept of "nation." So we talk of the United States as a unified entity and what "we as a nation" do. Such an approach overlooks the class dimensions of U.S. policy. Consider, for example, the question of foreign aid. It is misleading to say that the United States, as a nation, gives aid to this or that country. A nation as such does not give aid to another nation as such. More precisely, the common citizens of our country, through their taxes, give to the privileged elites of another country. As someone once said: foreign aid is when the poor people of a rich country give money to the rich people of a poor country. The transference is across class lines as well as national lines, representing an upward redistribution of income.

We hear talk about "our" interests abroad and "U.S. interests" in the world. But it's not easy to discover what "our" leaders mean by "U.S. interests." In 1967, during the Vietnam War, I first became aware of how often officials would refer to "U.S. interests" as a way of justifying their policies without ever pausing to tell us what those interests might be. I searched in vain through more than a dozen volumes of the *Department of State Bulletin,* looking for some definition or example of "U.S. interests." The closest I came was a comment by State Department official William Bundy, who cited "our vital military bases" in the Philippines as an essential U.S. interest. As often happens, an overseas military presence which is supposedly established to defend "our interests" (whatever they may be) itself becomes an interest to be defended. The instrumental value becomes an end value.

Bundy went on to indicate a "more important" interest than military bases. Speaking to an elite American and Filipino audience in Manila, he said, "The Philippines means so much to the United States because . . . this is a country where Americans are always, as Filipinos so often say, made to feel 'at home.'" If I understand Bundy, our interest in the Philippines was the preservation of Filipino hospitality.

Bundy's assertion had to overlook a great deal of imperialist history. From 1899 to 1902, some 200,000 Filipinos perished and tens of thousands others were wounded or tortured by U.S. forces in a successful effort to crush Filipino independence. Bundy also overlooked some grim present-day realities, including the mass poverty in the Philippines and the widespread prostitution industry conducted for the benefit of U.S. servicemen stationed there—giving new meaning to the idea of "made to feel 'at home.'"

The truth is "our interests" remain fuzzily defined because the term is used in a way that has nothing to do with our real interests. Nor does a change of administrations afford any clarification. During the 1992 presidential campaign, Bill Clinton vowed to chart a new course for our nation's future, reminding us that we must have the "courage to change." Fine sounding declarations. But once elected, Clinton remained in lockstep with his conservative

Republican predecessors, maintaining that the United States must remain a global superpower, that U.S. overseas involvement is always well-intentioned, and that "U.S. interests" could be supported by military force. And like his predecessors, he allowed no critical examination of what those interests might be.

Despite dramatic transformations throughout the world, Clinton invited no public debate on the subject of foreign policy. As a member of the Council on Foreign Relations, the Bilderberg Conference, and the Trilateral Commission, all corporate-dominated, elite policymaking bodies, Clinton was ideologically and personally part of the inner circle of power, not one to rock the boat, let alone change its course.

Consistent Inconsistencies

A common criticism of U.S. foreign policy is that it is often "self-contradictory." To the contrary, it is rigorously consistent in the class interests it advances. To illustrate the underlying coherence of apparently contradictory strategies, consider the treatment accorded Cuba and China. As of 1994, the U.S. government was continuing to pursue every stratagem short of war to cripple Cuba's economy, including travel and trade embargoes and reprisals against other nations or companies that try to trade with Havana. Many of the contracts Cuba negotiated with firms in other nations were canceled because of U.S. pressure. Washington's enmity was motivated by a desire to "restore" democracy and human rights in Cuba, we were told.

Critics were quick to note the "contradiction" in U.S. polices toward Cuba and China. They pointed out that China had committed numerous human rights violations, yet it was granted "most favored nation" trading status. Yet, officials called for "quiet diplomacy," assuring us that coercion would be counterproductive and that we could not impose a political litmus test on China, a strategy that was markedly different from the one used against Cuba.

But behind the apparent double standard rests the same underlying dedication to the forces of capital accumulation and a global status quo. China has opened itself to private capital and free market "reforms," including enterprise zones wherein corporate investors can superexploit the country's huge and cheap labor supply with no worry about restrictive regulations. In addition, because of its knee-jerk opposition to almost any political movement in the world that was friendly with the Soviets, China has supported the same counterrevolutionary and even fascist forces abroad as has the United States: Pinochet in Chile, the mujahideen in Afghanistan, Savimbi's UNITA in Angola, and the Khmer Rouge in Cambodia. In contrast, in each of those instances, Cuba was on the side of the forces that advocated social transformation. Thus, there is really no contradiction between U.S. policies toward Cuba and China—only in the rationales conjured to justify them.

Lacking a class perspective, all sorts of experts come to conclusions based on surface appearances. While attending a World Affairs Council meeting in San Francisco, I heard some participants refer to the irony of Cuba's having come "full circle" since the days before the revolution. In prerevolutionary Cuba, they pointed out, the best hotels and shops were reserved for the foreigners and the relatively few Cubans who had Yankee dollars. Today, it is the same.

This judgment overlooks some important differences. Strapped for hard currency, the revolutionary government decided to use its beautiful beaches and sunny climate to develop a tourist industry. By 1993, tourism had become Cuba's second most important source of hard currency income (after sugar). To be sure, tourists were given accommodations that few Cubans could afford since they did not have the dollars. But in prerevolutionary Cuba, the profits from tourism were pocketed by big corporations, generals, gamblers, and mobsters. Today the profits are split between the foreign investors who built the hotels and the Cuban government. The portion going to the government pays for health clinics, education, machinery, powdered milk, the importation of fuel, and the like. In other words, the people reap many of the benefits of the tourist trade—as is true of the export earnings from Cuban sugar, coffee, tobacco, rum, seafood, honey, and marble.

If Cuba were in exactly the same place as before the revolution, open to client-state servitude, Washington would have lifted the embargo. When the Cuban government no longer utilizes the public sector to redistribute a major portion of the surplus value to the common populace, and when it allows the productive surplus wealth to be pocketed by a few rich private owners and returns the factories and lands to a rich owning class—as the former communist nations of Eastern Europe have done—then it will have come full circle. Then it will be under client-state servitude and will be warmly embraced by Washington, as have other ex-communist nations.

U.S. refugee policy is another area criticized as "inconsistent." Cuban refugees regularly have been granted entry into this country while Haitian refugees are turned away. Of the 30,000 Haitians who applied for political asylum in 1993 only 783 were accepted. Since many Cubans are white and almost all Haitians are black, some people have concluded that the differences in treatment can only be ascribed to racism.

To be sure, ethnic discrimination has been embedded in U.S. immigration policy for most of the twentieth century, directed against Asians and Africans and to a lesser degree Eastern and Southern Europeans, and favoring Northern Europeans. But when considering the treatment of Cuban and Haitian refugees, we should look beyond skin color. Refugees from right-wing, client-state countries like El Salvador and Guatemala are Caucasian, yet they have great difficulty gaining asylum. Refugees from Nicaragua are of the same Latino stock as the Salvadorans and Guatemalans, yet they had relatively no trouble getting into the USA because they were considered to be fleeing a "communistic" Sandinista government. Refugees from Vietnam are Asian, but they have been granted entry into this country in large numbers, 35,000 in 1993 alone, because they too are fleeing an anticapitalist government.

During the Cold War, emigrés from the USSR and Eastern Europe were granted entrance visas as a matter of course. Now that communism has been replaced by conservative free-market governments, the State Department has the program "under review." In 1994, few Russians and almost no Ukrainians were granted visas, not even Jews, though the latter seem to be facing more anti-Semitic harassment than they ever did under communism.

In the above instances, the decisive consideration seemed to be not the complexion of the immigrants, but the political complexion of the governments in question. Generally, refugees from anticapitalist countries are automatically categorized as victims of political oppression and readily allowed entry, while refugees from politically repressive procapitalist countries are sent back, often to face incarceration or extermination. For if they are fleeing from a rightist procapitalist government, they are by definition politically undesirable.

By 1994, the refugee policy toward Cuba developed certain complications. In accordance with an earlier agreement between Havana and Washington, the Cuban government allowed people to leave for the United States if they had a U.S. visa. Washington had agreed to issue 20,000 visas a year but had in fact granted few, preferring to incite illegal departures and reap the propaganda value. All Cubans who fled illegally on skimpy crafts or hijacked vessels or planes were granted asylum in the USA and hailed as heroes who had risked their lives to flee Castro's tyranny. When Havana announced it would no longer play that game and would let anyone leave who wanted to, the Clinton administration reverted to a closed door policy, fearing an immigration tide. Now policymakers feared that the escape of too many disgruntled refugees would help Castro stay in power by easing tensions within Cuban society.

Cuba was condemned for not allowing its citizens to leave and then for allowing them to leave. But underlying this apparent inconsistency was Washington's desire to discredit the Cuban government for being a heartless oppressor. The goal, as stated by Deputy Assistant Secretary of State Michael Skol before a Congressional committee (March 17, 1994), is "the dismantling of the [Cuban] state." Political considerations take precedence over any regard for the plight of the people involved. To understand this, one needs to look beyond the immediate tactics to the overriding strategy.

Arms for Profit

Some critics charge that the huge U.S. military establishment is nothing but a wasteful boondoggle. They usually are the same people who say that U.S. foreign policy is stupid. Again, we would have to remind them that what may be wasteful and costly for one class (ordinary citizens and taxpayers) may be wonderful and rewarding for another (corporate defense contractors and military brass).

Over the years, some of us argued that were the Soviet Union and other communist countries to disappear, our leaders would still insist upon a huge military establishment. Reality rarely provides any opportunity to test a political hypothesis as in an experimental laboratory. In this instance, the hypothesis was put to the test when the communist governments were overthrown. Sure enough, the huge U.S. global military force remained largely intact, at a spending level far above what it was when the Cold War was at its height (even after adjusting for inflation).

Why so? First of all, military spending happens to be one of the greatest sources of domestic capital accumulation. It represents a form of public expenditure that business likes. When the government spends funds on the not-for-profit sector of the economy—such as the postal service, publicly-owned railroads, or affordable homes and public hospitals—it demonstrates how the public can create goods, services, and jobs and expand the tax base, without need of private investor gain. Such spending competes with the private market.

In contrast, missiles and aircraft carriers constitute a form of public expenditure that does not compete with the civilian market. A defense contract is like any other business contract, only better. The taxpayers' money covers all production risks. Unlike a refrigerator manufacturer who has to worry about selling his refrigerators, a weapons manufacturer has a product that already has been contracted, complete with guaranteed cost overruns. In addition, the government picks up most of the research and development costs.

Defense spending opens up an area of demand that is potentially limitless. How much military security or supremacy is enough? There are always new weapons that can be developed. The entire arms industry has a built-in obsolescence. Not long after a multibillion-dollar weapons system is produced, technological advances make it obsolete and in need of updating or replacement.

Furthermore, most military contracts are awarded without competitive bidding, so arms manufacturers pretty much get the price they ask for. Hence, the temptation is to develop weapons and supplies that are ever more elaborate and costly—and therefore ever more profitable. Such products are not necessarily the most efficient or sensible. Many perform poorly. But poor performance has its own rewards in the form of additional allocations to get weapons to work the way they should.

In sum, defense contractors enjoy a rate of return substantially higher than what is usually available on the civilian market. No wonder corporate leaders are in no hurry to cut military spending. What they have is a limitless, low-risk, high-profit, multibillion-dollar cornucopia. Arms spending bolsters the entire capitalist system, even as it impoverishes the not-for-profit public sector. These, then, are the two basic reasons why the United States assiduously remains an armed superpower even though lacking the pretext of an opposing superpower: First, a massive military establishment is needed to keep the world safe for global capital accumulation. Second, a massive military itself is a direct source of immense capital accumulation.

CHAPTER 6

DRUGS, LIES, AND VIDEO WARS

The reasons given to justify imperialist interventions are as numerous as they are contrived. As mentioned in the previous chapter, they include "defending democracy," "protecting U.S. interests," "fulfilling our responsibilities as world leader" and "containing the threat of Soviet global conquest." Here we examine additional pretexts.

Driving Away Demons

One way to convince Americans that their survival is threatened by an evil adversary is to personalize the evil. For years the top demon was the Soviet dictator Joseph Stalin. In the post–World War II era, critics of U.S. foreign policy, many of them conservatives, warned of overseas entanglements and the related dangers of inflation, big government, and runaway debt. In response, the cold warriors in Washington always had the dread specter of Stalin. Time and again, when it came time for Congress to vote, fiscal conservatism proved no match for the big-spending, budget-busting militarists and interventionists abetted by the image of Stalinist hoards ready to pounce upon us the moment we denied our armed forces a single ship or plane.

Besides the communists, the other designated demons were the populist nationalist leaders of the Third World. In 1952, for instance, there was Colonel Gamal Nasser of Egypt. He overthrew a corrupt, comprador monarchy and provided the Egyptian people with free public education for the first time in their history. Nasser laid claim to the Suez Canal, demanding that Egypt, rather than Great Britain and France, run it and collect the fees on its traffic. He also struck a nonaligned course in the Cold War. Such deviations from client-state subordination caused Secretary of State John Foster Dulles to brand President Nasser the "Hitler of the Nile" and a menace to the stability of the Middle East.

In 1957, the U.S. Congress approved a presidential resolution known as the "Eisenhower Doctrine," which designated the Middle East as an area vital to the national interest of the United States. As with the Monroe Doctrine and Truman Doctrine, "the U.S. government conferred upon the U.S. government the remarkable and enviable right to intervene militarily" in yet another region of the world, notes political analyst William Blum. Soon after, the CIA began operations to overthrow the democratically elected Syrian government and embarked upon a series of plots to eradicate Nasser and his irksome nationalism. If anyone was acting like a Hitlerite destabilizer in the Middle East, it was not President Nasser.

If we are to believe U.S. leaders and media pundits, Colonel Muammar Qaddafi of Libya is another demon, an "assassin" who is said to suffer from a "Hitlerite megalomania." Guest commentators on ABC's *Nightline* (December 4, 1981) also labeled him a "pathological liar" and a "madman." Qaddafi's real sin was that, in 1969, he overthrew a corrupt, obscenely rich ruling clique and moved toward a more egalitarian society, using a larger portion of its capital and labor for public needs. He also nationalized Libya's oil industry. Consequently, through much of the 1980s and 1990s, Libya was the object of U.S. provocations, air strikes, embargoes, and a protracted propaganda campaign designed to convince the American public that a country of three million, with a modestly equipped army of 55,000, had become a mortal threat to the United States.

Panama's president Manuel Noriega served as another demonized leader. In 1989, on the eve of the U.S. invasion of Panama, he was called "a wily jungle snake" and a "swamp rat" by TV news hosts. U.S. troops reportedly discovered voodoo paraphernalia, one hundred pounds of cocaine, and a portrait of Hitler among Noriega's possessions. Subsequent investigation ascertained that the voodoo implements turned out to be Indian carvings; the "cocaine" was an emergency stockpile of tortilla flour; and the picture of Hitler was in a *Time-Life* photo history of World War II.

The following year, Saddam Hussein underwent a similar demonization process, as the White House and the media revved up their propaganda war against Iraq. Saddam was called the "Butcher of Baghdad," a "madman," "psychologically deformed," and a "beast." President Bush described him as having done things that were "worse than Hitler." The leader of the targeted country is not only demonized but treated as a personification of his country. Having been equated with their leader, the nation's people are demonized by proxy and become fair game for any ensuing onslaught.

Looking Left for Terrorism

The demonized adversaries are often accused of terrorism. For years, the Reagan administration denounced the Soviets for running a worldwide terrorism network. Major news organizations like the *Washington Post* (January 27, 1981) concurred, accusing the Soviets and their allies of being the "principle source of terror in the world."

The *Wall Street Journal* (October 23, 1981) editorialized that the Soviets and Cubans had a "deep involvement in American terrorism." Books written by right-wing flacks like Claire Sterling asserted that Arab, Irish, Basque, Japanese, West German, and Italian terror groups were linked to Moscow. What was missing from all these charges was any shred of supporting evidence. (Nor was any corroboration forthcoming after the Soviet Union collapsed and KGB files were opened.)

The Libyans have been repeatedly charged with terrorism by U.S. officials. Most recently in the early 1990s, the U.S. government charged Libya with being behind the downing of Pan Am Flight 103 that crashed over Lockerbie, Scotland, killing 270 people, even though there was no material evidence implicating the Libyans and much to suggest that the perpetrators were linked to organizations in Iran and Syria.

In 1981, Libya was accused by the White House and its faithful flunkies in the news media of sending a hit team to kill the president. The news was saturated with hyped stories about the impending assassin attempt. Depending on what media source one believed, there were one or two hit teams, composed of three, five, ten, twelve, or thirteen assassins coming in from Canada or Mexico, composed of Libyans and Iranians, assisted perhaps by East Germans or Syrians or Lebanese or Palestinians. Never had a team of assassins received such advanced billing. It should have been enough to deter even the wildest publicity hounds among them. The nonexistent teams never materialized.

Meanwhile, real right-wing terrorist acts, like the bombing of a Cuban airliner that resulted in a great loss of life, a racist bombing of an interracial discotheque in West Germany, and hundreds of terrorist attacks and hate crimes *within* the United States by home-grown right-wing groups, directed against ethnic and religious minorities, gays, and abortion clinics, have caused hardly a ripple of concern in Washington.

By portraying itself as a champion against terror, the U.S. national security state deflects attention from its own international terror network, including the ex-Nazis who were sheltered in the United States and enlisted in terror campaigns in Latin America and elsewhere, and the military and paramilitary forces and death squads in dozens of countries—trained, equipped, and funded by the CIA and the Pentagon—that terrorize their own populations on a grand scale. In countries like Guatemala, Mozambique, and Haiti they killed more people in one week than Arab, Basque, and Northern Ireland "terrorist" groups killed in ten years.

Protecting Americans Abroad

The media frequently carry reports about Americans who end up in foreign jails. Invariably, a U.S. official appears in the story to warn our citizens that they must abide by the laws of the country they are visiting, and that, contrary to popular belief, they should not assume their government will be able to come to their rescue. But why do so many Americans have this mistaken impression?

Perhaps the answer is that there are two U.S. governments: the helpless one that shrugs and murmurs, "When you travel abroad, you're on your own"; and the other one that boldly proclaims, "We cannot sit by idly while U.S. lives are in danger; we're sending in the Marines." After more than a century of hearing the latter refrain, Americans can be forgiven for thinking that when abroad they are shielded by the full might and majesty of the United States.

"Protecting American lives" has been used repeatedly as an excuse to invade and occupy other countries. In 1958, to justify the landing of 10,000 U.S. Marines in Lebanon (sent there to save the procapitalist, comprador government from a nationalist uprising),

President Eisenhower claimed that U.S. citizens had to be evacuated to a safer place. In fact, they had been forewarned to avoid travel in Lebanon and most American civilians had departed that country well before the marines arrived.

In 1962, in the Dominican Republic, after thirty years of the U.S.-supported dictatorship of Rafael Trujillo, a free and fair election brought Juan Bosch to the presidency. Bosch called for land reform, low-rent housing, nationalization of some businesses, public works projects, a reduction in the import of luxury items, and civil liberties for all political groups. Washington held a jaundiced view of Bosch, seeing him as the purveyor of "creeping socialism." After only seven months in office, he was overthrown by the U.S.-backed Dominican military.

Three years after the coup, constitutionalist elements in the Dominican armed forces, abetted by armed civilians, rose up in an effort to restore Bosch to the presidency. During the ensuing struggle, the constitutionalist forces offered to cooperate fully in the evacuation of any U.S. nationals who wished to leave. In fact, no Americans were harmed nor did the White House seem concerned that any were at risk. But when it became apparent that the military junta would be ousted, President Lyndon Johnson sent in U.S. forces "to protect American lives." One might wonder why 23,000 troops were needed to rescue a relatively small number of Americans, none of whom were calling for help, some of whom were actually assisting the constitutionalists?

In fact, the invading force *was* engaged in a rescue operation— not of U.S. nationals but of the right-wing junta, supplying it with arms and funds, and directly participating in the bloody suppression of the constitutionalists. U.S. troops remained on the island for almost five months, long after any Americans might have needed to be evacuated. It was the fifth time in this century that the United

States had invaded the Dominican Republic to prevent popular social change and shore up the existing class autocracy.

In 1983, the familiar refrain of "American lives in danger" was played again when President Reagan invaded the tiny nation of Grenada (population 102,000), in an unprovoked assault, in violation of international law, killing scores of the island's defenders. The White House claimed the invasion was a rescue operation on behalf of American students at the St. George Medical School, who supposedly were endangered by the strife that had emerged between ruling factions on the island. In fact, as the school's chancellor testified, no students were threatened and few wanted to leave. After being warned of the impending invasion, many students changed their minds. Their desire to evacuate in order to be out of the way of a U.S. military action was now treated as justification for the action itself.

Grenada's real sin was that its revolutionary New Jewel movement had instituted a series of egalitarian reforms, including free grade school and secondary education, public health clinics (mostly with the assistance of Cuban doctors), and free distribution of foodstuffs to the needy along with materials for home improvements. The government also leased unused land to establish farm cooperatives, and sought to turn agriculture away from cash-crop exports and toward self-sufficient food production. After the invasion, these programs were abolished and unemployment and economic want increased sharply. The island had been prevented from persuing an alternative course of self-development.

A closing footnote: In the mid-1980s, as the Reagan administration hinted about invading Nicaragua, a large group of U.S. nationals in that country, who supported the Sandinista government, issued a statement making it clear that their lives were not threatened. So familiar was the pretext of "rescuing Americans," that they were anticipating its use by Washington and were trying to defuse a false issue.

Reaching for Pretexts

When individuals keep providing new and different explanations to justify a particular action, they most likely are lying. So with policymakers. In October 1917, the Russian Revolution sent tremors throughout the capitalist world. The Bolshevik party, with strong working-class support, overthrew the czarist autocracy, collectivized the landed estates, confiscated church property, nationalized the banks and private firms, and declared itself a workers' state. For the owning classes of the Western world, a nightmare had come true.

Within a matter of months, the United States and fourteen other capitalist nations invaded Soviet Russia. The U.S. public was told that (1) this military action was to prevent the Bolshevik government from aiding the Germans, with whom the Western allies were still at war. In fact, the Bolsheviks did make a separate peace with Germany but they showed no inclination to assist the Kaiser. Once the war with Germany ended, a new excuse was required. President Woodrow Wilson now proclaimed that (2) the invading troops were needed to reestablish order and prevent atrocities. He conveniently overlooked the fact that it was the interventionists and their White Guard allies who were causing most of the disorder and committing most of the atrocities. Then it was said that (3) the intervention was to get the Bolsheviks to pay back the monies that the previous czarist regime had borrowed from Europe.

Eventually, President Wilson admitted the real reason: (4) he could not abide the Bolsheviks. But he never explained what was so insufferable about them. The real intent of the allied intervention was to overthrow the newly emerging, avowedly anticapitalist order. The first successful proletarian revolution in history had to be undone, lest it serve as a dangerous example to the common people in other nations, including the United States. Leaders like Secretary cf State Lansing and Wilson himself expressed this apprehension in their private correspondence. But never did they tell the common people in this or any other capitalist country what really concerned them.

The grabbing for alibis was much in evidence during the Vietnam War in the 1960s. In the early stages of the conflict, Washington officials said U.S. involvement was necessary (1) to stabilize the government of South Vietnam. Then it was (2) to prevent an invasion from North Vietnam. As the casualties piled up, the purported policy goal was (3) to save all of Southeast Asia from "Asian communism with its headquarters in Peiking." In the last years of the war, the professed stakes were nothing less than (4) the security and national honor of the United States and the survival of the Free World.

Turning to Grenada, we noted earlier how the Reagan administration used (1) rescuing American medical students as the excuse for an invasion. Reagan then claimed that (2) Grenada had built up an immense arms arsenal that could threaten other Caribbean nations, and (3) had become an instrument of Soviet power by building a port to harbor Soviet submarines and a military airport for Soviet planes—all untrue. We were also told that (4) the island abutted a vulnerable "choke point" in our shipping routes; in other words, tiny Grenada might have brought the United States to its knees by cutting off its sea lanes. Once in control of the island, the invaders instituted a "free market" government headed by a U.S.-financed New National party, thereby achieving the real purpose of the invasion: to prevent any nation in the Caribbean from removing itself from the global corporate system.

Official pronouncements regarding the U.S.-backed Contra war against Nicaragua in the 1980s revealed a similar pattern of escalating pretexts. Initially we were told that the attacks were intended (1) to interdict the arms that Managua was sending to the Salvadoran rebels. It was never explained why the Salvadoran FMLN should not be assisted in its struggle against a murderous dictatorship. Then we were told that intervention against Managua was designed (2) to induce the Nicaraguans to hold democratic elections—something they had already done in 1984. Then it was (3) to prevent Nicaragua from becoming a Soviet satellite. Finally, it was (4) to stop Nicaragua from exporting its revolution to all of Central America and menacing the security of the United States itself. The rationales tend to escalate as the intervention grows in scope and cost.

The Gulf War massacre of 1991 is a prime example of how lies and war go hand in hand. In late 1989, after receiving assurances from U.S. officials that Washington would remain neutral, Iraq invaded Kuwait. In response, the Bush administration, assisted by other U.N. member nations, launched a month of intensive aerial assaults on the Iraqi occupation force in Kuwait and on civilian populations in Iraq, including the city of Baghdad.

After discussions with the Soviet Union, Iraq agreed to withdraw from Kuwait over a three-week period. But President Bush would give them only a week. The Iraqi evacuation was turned into a U.S. aerial slaughter of the retreating troops. Over 100,000 Iraqis, including many civilians, were killed in the one-sided conflict. There were a few hundred U.S. casualties.

The Gulf War (or "Desert Storm," as it was called by officials) demonstrated that a foreign leader need not be a communist to feel the full brunt of U.S. imperialism. Although Saddam brought a better-than-average standard of living to his people and pursued policies of national development, he manifested few of the ideological egalitarian impulses that defenders of capitalism find so loathsome. He tortured and murdered large numbers of communists and other left dissidents, a policy that usually makes Washington feel all warm and fuzzy toward any dictator. Until shortly before the Gulf War, Saddam was a regular recipient of U.S. military aid. So why did President Bush come down so hard on Iraq?

The Gulf War Lies

The initial excuse given by the Bush administration was that (1) U.S. forces were needed in the Middle East to defend Saudi Arabia from an impending Iraqi invasion. But if the Iraqis intended to take Saudi Arabia, why did they not move into that country immediately after grabbing Kuwait and well before U.S. troops arrived? Contrary to the disinformation passed around, journalists could find no Iraqi troops massed on the Saudi border.

Bush claimed that his attack came only after "months of constant and virtually endless diplomatic activity," and that (2) Iraq displayed no interest in a negotiated settlement. This was an outright lie. In the one "diplomatic" session held with the Iraqis by Secretary of State Baker in Geneva, he simply ordered them to leave Kuwait. By his own account, Baker made no effort to explore Iraq's grievances with Kuwait. When the Iraqis floated peace feelers through the remainder of 1990, they were ignored by the White House.

The Bush administration was spoiling for the one-sided fight. White House spokespersons were quoted as describing an Iraqi withdrawal from Kuwait as "the nightmare scenario." Why so? Would not the avoidance of war have been a dream scenario? The policymakers understood that a peaceful withdrawal would remove the casus belli and deprive the president of "a glorious victory against aggression."

The president also claimed he was concerned with (3) protecting human rights in Kuwait and elsewhere in the Middle East. But there was precious little democracy in any of the region's feudal emirates and autocracies. In Saudi Arabia, women were still stoned to death on charges of adultery. In Kuwait, democratic councils and other organized political groupings were regularly crushed. One filthy-rich family controlled the country's politico-economic life.

It was also maintained that (4) the United States was upholding the United Nations commitment to defend member states against aggression. But why only in this instance? Both Syria and Israel invaded Lebanon and still occupied portions of that country; Turkey grabbed half of Cyprus; Morocco waged a war of aggression against the Western Sahara; Indonesia invaded and annexed East Timor at a great loss of Timorese lives. Yet Washington maintained close and supportive relations with all these aggressors. When Iraq invaded Iran, a few years before the Gulf War, Washington sent military aid to both countries. U.S. leaders themselves invaded Grenada and Panama. One can look with skepticism on Washington's sudden and highly principled intolerance of aggression.

In August 1990, Bush asserted that (5) he was trying to prevent Saddam from monopolizing "all the world's great oil reserves." This alibi at least brought us closer to the truth: oil was definitely a consideration. But the charge was false. No single producer can control the global oil market, not even a powerful consortium like OPEC, let alone an individual leader like Saddam. Even with the 1990 embargo that cut off the oil from Iraq, the world's net petroleum production remained roughly the same.

The White House then charged that (6) Iraq posed a nuclear threat. This polemic was tacked on to Bush's list of pretexts months after he had embarked upon intervention and immediately after opinion polls showed that Americans responded apprehensively to the possibility of Iraq's developing a nuclear capability. In any case, with sanctions in place, it was impossible for Iraq to get the necessary materials to build a nuclear bomb.

In November 1990, Secretary Baker argued that (7) the intervention would safeguard jobs at home. This was the first time anyone in Bush's national security entourage had evinced concern for the nation's work force. Nobody specified how a costly massacre in the Middle East would protect jobs at home. In fact, after the war, unemployment increased slightly. Besides, there were more effective and less horrible ways of keeping Americans employed than wreaking destruction upon another nation.

Some Real Reasons

There were a number of compelling considerations for war against Iraq that the Bush administration preferred to leave unmentioned. First, Saddam Hussein was trying to stop the Kuwaiti slant drilling into his oil reserves and was trying to bolster the oil price he could get. His temerity in putting considerations about his own country's economy ahead of the interests of the international oil cartel suddenly made him an unpopular personage in Washington.

Second, thanks to the major networks, the Gulf War served as a video promotional event for the military-industrial complex, a rescue operation for a bloated defense budget. In July 1990, for the first time in years, the Democratic leadership in Congress was talking about real cuts in military spending. The Gulf War hoopla brought Congress meekly back into line.

Third, the quick and easy victory was a promotional event for interventionism itself, a cure for the "Vietnam syndrome" (that is, the public's unwillingness to commit U.S. forces to violent conflicts abroad). The Gulf War seemed to solve a problem U.S. interventionists long have faced: how to engage in military action without a serious loss of American lives. (Their concern was more political than humanitarian. Heavy losses make the intervention unpopular with the U.S. public.) The way to economize on American lives was to apply an air, land, and sea firepower of such superior magnitude that it could destroy the opponent's military capacity, infrastructure, and life support systems without any great commitment of U.S. troops.

It is not true, as was claimed by antiwar activists, that Iraq was bombed back into the nineteenth century. Iraq in the nineteenth century had a productive base roughly commensurate with the population needs of that time. The destruction created a far greater crisis than that. In March 1991, a United Nations mission to Iraq reported that the conflict "has wrought near-apocalyptic results" by destroying "most means of modern life support," relegating Iraq "to a preindustrial age, but with all the disabilities of post-industrial dependency on intensive use of energy and technology."

Not without cause did U.S. militarists boast that the attacks were "surgical." True, most of the bombs were free-falling and killed people wantonly. But the thousands of air strikes did surgically remove most of Iraq's electrical systems and seriously damaged the agricultural system. Without electricity, water could not be purified, sewage could not be treated. Hunger, cholera, and other diseases flourished.

The Gulf War was followed by a vindictive United Nations embargo that several years later still denied Iraq the technological resources to rebuild its food production, medical services, and sanitation facilities. As late as 1993, CNN reported that nearly 300,000 Iraqi children were suffering from malnutrition. Deaths exceeded the normal rate by 125,000 a year, mostly affecting "the poor, their infants, children, chronically ill, and elderly" (*Los Angeles Times,* February 22, 1994). Iraqi citizens, who previously had enjoyed a decent living standard, were reduced to destitution. So was realized one of the perennial goals of imperialism: to reduce to impotence and poverty all potential adversaries and upstarts.

Fourth, the Gulf crisis allowed U.S. leaders to establish a long-term military presence in the Middle East, a region of troubled regimes and abundant oil reserves. U.S. forces now could more immediately and effectively safeguard existing autocracies from their own restive populations.

Fifth, many wars are begun, noted Alexander Hamilton in *Federalist* No. 6, because of the political interests of leaders. By plunging into conflicts abroad, they seek to diminish the impact of troublesome issues at home, thereby securing their political fortunes. The war against Iraq came in the middle of a serious recession, one that President Bush was more interested in ignoring than resolving. In July 1990, his popularity also was slumping badly because of the savings and loan scandal. Every evening, TV news programs were peeling off successive layers of corruption, thievery, bribery, and plunder of the public treasury, in what was the greatest financial conspiracy in the history of the world. But once the media became preoccupied with selling the high-tech video war, the savings and loan issue was dropped from the evening news. The Gulf victory also made it harder to investigate disclosures implicating Bush in the Iran-Contra conspiracy, as he basked in what seemed like an untouchable popularity.

While the war was still in progress, I wrote in *CovertAction Information Bulletin* (Spring 1991): "The morning after victory, more of the American public may begin to wonder if the bloodshed and the $80 billion bill was worth it. They might recall that the only war worth supporting is what Benjamin Franklin called 'the best war,' the one that is never fought." Indeed, the slaughter perpetrated against Iraq and all its attendant hoopla were not enough to carry Bush to reelection the following year.

The "War On Drugs": Cover Story

Among the various crusades fabricated by our leaders is the "war on drugs." On Pacifica Radio (October 31, 1990), a spokesperson from America Watch described how the United States was giving funds to military and paramilitary groups in Colombia ostensibly to stop the narcotics traffic. Instead, these forces were devoting their efforts to torturing and killing members of the legal Left, those working for social reform and a peaceful electoral challenge. The America Watch representative concluded that "unfortunately" U.S. policy "is in error." In its haste to fight the war on drugs, Washington was "giving money to the wrong people."

Actually, the administration was giving money to the right people, who were putting it to exactly the use Washington desired. Again it was assumed that U.S. leaders were misguided when in fact they were misguiding us. Colombia was the leading human rights violator in the hemisphere and, under the Clinton administration, the leading recipient of U.S. military aid.

In Peru, too, under the guise of fighting drug trafficking, U.S. forces became deeply involved in a political counterinsurgency that has taken thousands of lives. U.S. funds have been used to train and equip Peruvian troops, who have been put to merciless use in areas suspected of cooperating with insurgent guerrillas.

The White House would have us believe that the purpose of the 1989 invasion of Panama was to apprehend President Manuel Noriega, because he had dealt in drugs and was therefore in violation of U.S. laws. Here the United States operated under the remarkable principle that its domestic laws had jurisdiction over what the heads of foreign nations did in their own countries. Were that rule to work both ways, a U.S. president could be seized and transported to a fundamentalist Islamic country to be punished for failing to observe its laws.

U.S. forces did more than go after Noriega. They bombed and forcibly evacuated working-class neighborhoods in Panama City that were pro-Noriega strongholds. They arrested thousands of officials, political activists, and journalists, and purged the labor unions and universities of anyone of leftist orientation. They installed a government headed by rich compradors, such as President Guillermo Endara, who were closely connected to companies, banks, and individuals deeply involved in drug operations and the laundering of drug money.

The amount of narcotics that came through Panama represented but a small fraction of the total flow into the United States. The real problem with Panama was that it was a populist-nationalist government. The Panamanian Defense Force was a left-oriented military. General Omar Torrijos, Noriega's predecessor who was killed in a mysterious plane explosion that some blame on the CIA, initiated a number of egalitarian social programs. The Torrijos government also negotiated a Canal treaty that was not to the liking of U.S. right-wingers. And Panama maintained friendly relations with Cuba and Sandinista Nicaragua. Noriega had preserved most of Torrijos's reforms.

After the U.S. invasion, unemployment in Panama soared; the public sector was cut drastically; and pension rights and other work benefits were abolished. Today Panama is once more a client-state nation, in the iron embrace of the U.S. empire.

Which Side Are You On, Boys?

The U.S. national security state has done nothing to stop the international drug trade and much to assist it. Some people quip that "CIA" stands for "Capitalism's International Army." Others say it stands for "Cocaine Import Agency." In Laos in the early 1960s, the agency lived up to both names. The CIA's biggest asset in recruiting the Meo tribes into an army to fight against the anti-imperialist, anti-capitalist Pathet Lao was its ability to transport the Meo's big cash crop of opium out of remote villages onto major markets via Air America, a CIA-operated airline.

When this story became public, the CIA admitted knowing that the Meo were transporting opium on Air America and claimed it had tried to stop them from doing it, but, well, it wasn't easy. In fact, CIA pilots subsequently reported they were under orders from their superiors not to interfere with the shipments. As Alfred McCoy documented, opium production by CIA-backed warlords in Southeast Asia increased tenfold soon after the CIA moved in.[1]

As early as 1947–1950, the CIA enlisted Sicilian and Corsican mafia to break longshoremen strikes by communist-led unions in France and Italy, providing them with money and arms. In exchange, the syndicates were given a free hand in the transport of heroin, much of which ended up in the United States.

In 1980 in Bolivia, the CIA helped overthrow a democratically elected, reformist government and install a rightist military junta. Marked by mass arrests, torture, and killings, the takeover became known as "the Cocaine Coup" in recognition of how the new rulers openly cooperated with Bolivia's cocaine lords.

In 1988, witnesses before Senator Kerry's Senate Subcommittee on Terrorism, Narcotics, and International Operations gave evidence of a massive drug operation in which CIA and other government personnel were involved, along with top executive and military leaders of a number of Latin American countries. CIA operatives were using the funds accumulated from drug trafficking to subsidize counterrevolutionary armies throughout the region and in some cases were lining their own pockets.

A former intelligence aid to Noriega, José Blandon, told the Kerry Committee that the Costa Rican airstrips used for arms deliveries to the Nicaraguan Contras also carried cocaine shipments to the United States. An official investigative committee in Costa Rica brought charges against John Hull, an American rancher who was linked to the CIA and the drug trade. Costa Rican authorities requested (unsuccessfully) that Hull be extradited, charging that he had been involved in murder and in smuggling arms and drugs into their country. Complicit with him, they named Lieutenant Colonel

---

1. Alfred McCoy, *The Politics of Heroin: CIA Complicity in the Globe Drug Trade* (New York: Lawrence Hill Books, 1991).

Oliver North and Rob Owen, former legislative assistant to then-senator Dan Quayle of Indiana. Hull was also implicated in criminal fraud, obstruction of justice, and trafficking in this country, yet the Justice Department took no action against him. Nor was he extradicted to Costa Rica.

In 1989, an agent of the Drug Enforcement Administration in El Salvador, Celerino Castillo III, gave a detailed account of a huge drug and arms smuggling operation that had been run by Oliver North's network and the CIA out of a military airport in El Salvador, which Castillo had uncovered. At a press conference in Washington, D.C., August 2, 1994, Castillo reiterated his belief that North knew narcotics were being run out of the air base in Ilopango: "All his pilots were drug traffickers. He knew what they were up to and refused to do anything about it." Edwin Corr, then-U.S. ambassador to El Salvador, told Castillo that it was "a covert White House operation run by Col. Oliver North and for us to stay away from [it]" (*San Francisco Weekly,* May 18, 1994). Both the Kerry committee report and Independent Counsel Lawrence Walsh's final report on Iran-Contra contain critical evidence against North, who instead of going to prison went on to run for the U.S. Senate.

The Costa Rican indictment against Hull and the charges against North received almost no attention in the mainstream media, just a few ho-hum lines on an inside page of the *New York Times.* If a progressive leader like Jesse Jackson had been linked to the Sandinistas in narcotics and arms trade, it would have played as a major story for weeks on end. If the war against drugs is being lost, it is because the national security state is on the side of the traffickers.

Drugs as a Weapon of Social Control

Besides financing wars and lining pockets, narcotics are useful as an instrument of social control. As drugs became more plentiful in the

United States, consumption increased dramatically. Demand may create supply, but supply also creates demand. The first condition for consumption is availability, getting the product before the public in plentiful amounts. Forty years ago, inner-city communities were just as impoverished as they are now, but they were not consuming drugs at the present level because narcotics were not pouring into them in such abundance and at such accessible prices as today.

Those who want to legalize marijuana should specify "marijuana" instead of using the general term "drugs," because to many people drugs means crack, ice, PCBs, heroin, and other hard stuff that has taken a serious toll on their communities.

A successful international war on drugs would not be impossible if the United States made a concerted effort, and if it got countries like Pakistan, Afghanistan, Thailand, Colombia, Peru, and Bolivia to be as tough on their drug traffickers as they are on their peasants, students, and workers who struggle for social betterment.

U.S. policy is less concerned with fighting a war against drugs than in using drugs and drug traffickers in the empire's eternal war for social control at home and abroad. Like the ex-Nazis who proved useful in the war against communism, the drug traffickers (some of whom are linked to fascist organizations) are on the side of the CIA. "For the CIA to target international drug networks," write Peter Dale Scott and Jonathan Marshall in *Cocaine Politics* (1991), "it would have to dismantle prime sources of intelligence, political leverage, and indirect financing for its Third World operations." This would be nothing less than "a total change of institutional direction."

While talking big about fighting drugs, President Reagan cut one-third of the federal law enforcement funds for fighting organized crime. The Drug Enforcement Agency was reduced 12 percent, causing the dismissal of 434 DEA employees, including 211 agents.

The Coast Guard was downsized, resulting in less coastal surveillance of illicit traffic. The U.S. Attorney's staff was cut drastically, creating a shortage of lawyers and causing the Justice Department to drop 60 percent of its drug and crime cases. All this moved crime investigator Dan Moldea to describe the Reagan drug policy as "a fraud." And Congressman Tom Lewis complained, "We're just arresting ponies, the little people. Why aren't we getting the big guys?"

The Bush administration restored none of the Reagan cuts and developed no new strategies to make the war against drugs a real one. In fact, Bush reduced the already sparse U.S. Border Patrol, causing the *New York Times* (August 27, 1989) to conclude, "The Bush Administration's proposed budget for the fiscal year 1990 would result in even fewer [anti-drug] agents along the border." As in so many other areas of public policy, the Clinton administration did nothing of note in the war against drugs.

In the mid-nineteenth century, when the British introduced great quantities of opium into China, it was not in response to a demand by the Chinese. For the British, it was a devilishly convenient way of creating a new market and turning a good profit on something produced in one colony (India), while propagating quiescence among a potentially explosive population in another colony (China). The Opium Wars were an attempt by the Chinese to resist the British-sponsored drug traffic. The Chinese knew that to "just say no" was not enough. They also knew that legalization was not the solution, for, in effect, the British had legalized the drug trade—and that was the problem.

One need not be a conspiracy theorist to wonder if right-wing policymakers are not playing the same kind of game with the drug traffic in this country. The protest organizations that arose in African American and Latino communities during the 1960s were systematically destroyed by police and federal authorities, their leaders killed or jailed on trumped-up charges. Soon after, the drug dealers moved in to complete the demoralization of those communities. They were undeterred by federal authorities who allowed shipments to pour into the country. Instead of mobilizing and fighting effectively for bread and butter issues, today's inner-city residents have been fighting for their lives against drug infestation.

Those who argue that we could cure the drug problem by legalizing it overlook the fact that in practice it already *is* legalized, and that is the problem. It flows into communities with little opposition from law enforcers and often with their active collaboration. The police frequently are in the pay of drug lords and are more likely to act against citizens who resist the narcotics traffic than against the traffickers themselves.

Some conservative commentators, such as William Buckley, Jr., advocate legalization of drugs, contradictorily claiming that the drug problem is not that serious and at the same time vastly uncontrollable because it is so widespread. These conservatives, who rail against the corrosion of American values, seem oddly languid about the destructive effects of narcotics. Understandably, they are far more willing to see low-income youths immobilized by drug infestation than mobilized to struggle for a popular redistribution of public resources. They prefer that inner-city youth not talk revolution—as did their counterparts of an earlier generation who joined the Young Lords, the Blackstone Rangers, and the Black Panthers—but keep busy instead shooting themselves up with needles and each other with guns.

When street leaders work for peace between the gangs and try to move their energies in an organized political direction, they run into more repression from the law than when they indulge in the usual gang activities.[2] Drugs are an important instrument of repression and social control. The British imperialists knew it and so do conservative pundits, the police, the CIA, and the White House. From Harlem to Honduras, the empire uses every device within its grasp to keep restive peoples demoralized and disorganized.

---

2. One example: In 1994 former Los Angeles gang leader-cum-community leader and chief peacemaker Dewayne Holmes was railroaded into jail on the trumped-up charge of stealing $10 from someone who was causing a disturbance at a dance that Holmes had organized. He is serving seven years. For details, see Christian Parenti, "Founder of Gang Truce Framed," *Z Magazine,* November 1993.

CHAPTER 7

WORTHY CAUSES

Mainstream apologists maintain that "we" have intervened in other countries for a number of worthy causes, such as discouraging weapons proliferation, carrying out humanitarian missions, and establishing electoral democracies. Let us scrutinize these assertions.

Discouraging Arms Proliferation

We have been told that the United States is a force for peace and against arms proliferation. In fact, U.S. arms manufacturers and the Pentagon have given us missiles with million-dollar computers built into them to guide them to their targets; nonnuclear "monster" bombs, each with enough explosive capacity to destroy whole neighborhoods; helicopter gunships, each with more firepower than a battalion of conventionally armed troops; armor-piercing antitank projectiles whose cores are made from radioactive nuclear waste (thousands of which, used in the Gulf War, have contaminated the soil and groundwater in Kuwait and Iraq with uranium depletion, causing cancer among the civilian population).

Hardly a nation in the Third World is not armed to the teeth with weapons developed and distributed by U.S. defense contractors, working hand in glove with the Pentagon to maintain about $20 billion a year in sales abroad. U.S. arms manufacturers now sell the technology to produce weapons as well as the weapons themselves. Countries like Turkey, South Korea, Indonesia, Taiwan, Israel, Egypt, Argentina, and Singapore are producing a wide range of modern military systems with assistance from U.S. firms. A number of these countries have become arms exporters on their own.

In regard to nuclear weapons, the United States was the first to develop the atom bomb and the only one ever to use it—at Hiroshima and Nagasaki in 1945. The Eisenhower administration offered nuclear weapons to the French on the eve of their Dienbienphu defeat in Indochina in 1954; Paris declined the offer. The Eisenhower administration threatened a nuclear strike against China in 1955, when Peking made moves against Quemoy and Matsu, two tiny offshore islands used by the Nationalist Chinese to launch attacks against the mainland. U.S. decisionmakers hinted about using nuclear weapons in Vietnam during the 1960s and early 1970s and against the Soviet Union during the Cuban missile crisis in 1962.

From 1945 through 1990, the U.S. national security state exploded at least 950 nuclear bombs, or one detonation every eighteen days, more than all other nations combined. The U.S. military has the largest fleet of long-range nuclear bombers, including the B-52, FB-111, and B-1B. As if these were not enough, Congress voted an additional $31 billion to buy fifteen B-2 Stealth bombers in 1990. The U.S. military possesses thousands of strategic and tactical missiles armed with some 17,000 nuclear warheads. About 4,500 nuclear weapons are deployed with American forces overseas. This arsenal supposedly was needed to deter a Soviet attack. But it remains largely intact to this day.

U.S. officials present themselves as opposed to nuclear build-ups—in certain other countries. On the flimsiest of evidence, they have charged Iran and then Iraq with developing a "nuclear capability," then treated this possibility as an imminent threat to "regional peace and stability." When Cuba announced plans to construct a nonmilitary nuclear plant, Washington made noises about that country's "potential nuclear capability."

In 1993, the CIA and the Pentagon charged that the Democratic People's Republic of Korea (DPRK), better known as communist North Korea, was engaged in a clandestine nuclear weapons program. As evidence, they pointed to its routine extraction of plutonium rods from nuclear installations. Unmentioned by U.S. officials and news media was that between May 1992 and January 1993, the DPRK had allowed six on-site inspections by the International Atomic Energy Agency (IAEA). In an interview on CNN (April 16, 1994) DPRK president Kim Il Sung insisted that his country had neither the capacity nor intent to build nuclear arms: "The world is now calling on our country to show nuclear weapons we don't have. . . . We have done a lot of construction in our country and we don't want to destroy it. Those who want war are out of their minds." In a subsequent interview with a representative of the Carnegie Endowment for International Peace, Kim added, "What would be the point of our making one or two nuclear weapons when you have 10,000, plus delivery systems that we don't have."

Washington advocated economic sanctions against Pyongyang and secured adoption of an IAEA resolution that demanded an inspection of all North Korean military sites. This was followed by a joint military exercise of 200,000 U.S. and South Korean troops, with weapons that included nuclear arms. In response, the North put its forces on alert and stated:

> Some officials of the IAEA secretariat insist stubbornly on the "inspection" of our military bases as dictated by the United States, while ignoring our demand for inspection of the nuclear weapons and nuclear bases of the United States in South Korea. If we submissively accept an unjust inspection by the IAEA, it would be to legitimize the espionage acts of the United States . . . and lead to the beginning of the full exposure of all our military installations.

In a NBC-TV interview (April 3, 1994), Defense Secretary William Perry remarked chillingly, "It's conceivable where [U.S.] actions might provoke North Koreans into unleashing a war and that is a risk we're willing to take." Perry's predecessor, Les Aspin, had noted, "Our focus is on the need to project power into regions important to our interests and to defeat potentially hostile regional powers such as North Korea and Iraq." In May 1994, Senator John McCain (R-Ariz.), considered an influential voice on foreign policy, called for air strikes on a DPRK nuclear reactor in Yongban, even though he admitted it "could cause the release of nuclear radiation." Pyongyang could be forgiven for thinking it was being targeted. Left unmentioned throughout the controversy was that the United States, according to a 1986 Brookings Institution estimate, had one thousand nuclear weapons in South Korea within easy striking distance of North Korea.

Washington's campaign to stop the proliferation of nuclear weapons has been applied in a politically selective way against countries it has wanted to destabilize: Iraq, Iran, Cuba, the Soviet Union, Libya, and North Korea. The nuclear arsenals of countries whose policies are congruent with those of the U.S. global empire, such as Great Britain, France, Pakistan, and pre-1994 South Africa, have evoked no alarm in Washington.

At the very time it was portraying North Korea as a nuclear threat, the Clinton administration completely disregarded Japan's stockpiling of plutonium in violation of international accords. No U.S. leader has voiced anxiety about Israel or China, though each has about two hundred nuclear bombs. The United States even helped provide material assistance to Israel and South Africa when they were engaged in building their thermonuclear weapons.

In sum, the U.S. "nonproliferation" policy rests on a hypocritical double standard. If U.S. leaders really were interested in promoting worldwide denuclearization, they would drastically reduce the U.S. arsenal and vigorously advocate a nonproliferation policy for all countries.

Chemical Warfare Hoax

After refusing for fifty years to sign the Geneva Protocol, which prohibits the use of chemical and biological warfare (CBW), the United States became a signatory in 1975. Soon after, U.S. officials claimed to have "overwhelming" evidence that the Soviets (who signed the Protocol in 1928) had been waging chemical war in Afghanistan, Cambodia, and Laos. If true, the charge would have given Washington enough justification to continue expanding its own CBW program. Leading American mycotoxin and CBW specialists questioned the charges, noting among other things that:

1. Massive chemical war campaigns extending over nine years and killing thousands of people would have produced more than the few fungus-ridden leaves and twigs offered up by Washington. There would have been hundreds of foliage samples, many contaminated corpses, a large number of duds, shell fragments, and gas canisters with heavy traces of mycotoxin.

2. The government's description of the delivery systems used by the Soviets (balloons and shells emitting clouds, tanks spraying liquids) fit no known type of chemical or biological attack system.

3. Descriptions of victims vomiting great quantities of blood were implausible insofar as no vomiting of blood has ever been found in decades of laboratory experiments with animals.

In 1984, two U.S. scientists announced that "yellow rain" residues in Southeast Asia were not CBW deposits but massive amounts of bee excrement. They decided that the U.S. government was guilty of nothing more than "sloppy research" and "honest error." This implausible conclusion was given wide play in the media and has been accepted even among people on the Left. Once again, it was presumed that policymakers were stupid rather than mendacious. We were asked to believe that throughout their decade-long disinformation campaign, they just kept mistaking bee feces for chemical attacks, that when they fabricated vivid "eye-witness" reports about Soviet rockets emitting not only yellow but red and green clouds of poisonous gas, and when they produced unsubstantiated testimonies of "victims" who claimed to have been poisoned in CBW attacks, and the many other contrived stories about Soviet chemical warfare, all this was just the result of an "honest error" about bee excrement. In fact, it was what it was, a concerted disinformation campaign that repeatedly utilized false props, fabricated testimonies, imaginary scenarios, and every other deliberate contrivance.

In 1988, Washington turned its sights on Libya, claiming that aerial photographs revealed that Colonel Qaddafi had built a chemical plant with the intention of producing CBW weapons. Qaddafi maintained that the factory was not equipped for CBW production and offered to allow an international inspection of its premises. U.S. leaders rejected the offer, saying a one-time inspection would not prove that the plant might not *someday* be used for chemical weapons—in effect admitting that their aerial photos could not validate their accusations.

In 1991 during the Gulf War, U.S. officials justified an air attack on a factory in Iraq by claiming that it had been secretly manufacturing chemical weapons. Subsequent investigation, including testimony from the European firm involved in the original construction of the plant, demonstrated that it had been producing powdered milk for children, as the Iraqis had asserted.

Humanitarian Pretense

Contrary to popular belief, the United States is no different from most other countries in that it does not have a particularly impressive humanitarian record. True, many nations, including our own, have sent relief abroad in response to particular crises. But these actions do not represent essential foreign policy commitments. They occur sporadically, are limited in scope, and obscure the many occasions when governments choose to do absolutely nothing for other countries in desperate straits.

Most U.S. aid missions serve as pretexts for hidden political goals, namely, to bolster conservative regimes, build infrastructures that assist big investors, lend an aura of legitimacy to counterinsurgency programs, and undermine local agrarian self-sufficiency while promoting U.S. agribusiness.

There have been memorable occasions when U.S. officials showed themselves to be anything but humanitarian. Consider the Holocaust. The Roosevelt administration did virtually nothing to accommodate tens of thousands of Jews who sought to escape extermination at the hands of the Nazis. Washington refused to ease its restrictive immigration quotas and would not even fill the limited number of slots allotted to Jews. U.S. officials even went so far as to persuade Latin American governments to close their doors to European immigration.

Consider South Africa. For decades Washington did nothing to discourage that white racist-dominated country from inflicting misery and death upon its African population. U.S. leaders preferred to maintain trade and investment relations with the apartheid regime. It lifted not a single humanitarian finger to stop the West Pakistani massacre of East Pakistan (later renamed Bangladesh). It was more concerned with preventing India and the Soviet Union from extending their influence in the region. In the 1980s, the U.S. national security state quietly assisted the Khmer Rouge in their campaigns of mayhem and murder, using them as a destabilizing force against the socialist government in Cambodia.

Be it the indigenous rain forest peoples of South America and Southeast Asia, or the Kurds, Biafrans, or Palestinians, be it overseas Chinese in Indonesia, East Timorese, Angolans, Mozambicans, Guatemalans, Salvadorans, or dozens of other peoples, the United States has done little to help rescue them from their terrible plights, and in most instances has done much to assist their oppressors.

For Freedom, Mujahideen Style

Some have pointed to Afghanistan as an example of a good intervention, the rescuing of an embattled people from Soviet aggression. In fact, the destabilizer in Afghanistan was not Moscow but the U.S. national security state. Years before Soviet troops entered the country, the Carter administration was providing assistance to Afghan tribes rebelling against the Kabul government. Kabul had a nonaggression pact with Moscow and received Soviet military and economic aid. In the late 1970s, the Afghan military embarked upon a social revolution that included programs in land reform, literacy, housing, and public health.

The privileged landowners and mujahideen tribesmen—based mostly in Iran and Pakistan—accelerated their rebellion, assisted by billions of dollars in aid from the United States and Saudi Arabia. For the feudal landowners, the insufferable feature of the revolutionary government was its land reform program on behalf of tenant farmers. For the tribesmen, it was the government's dedication to gender equality and the education of women and children, and the campaign to abolish opium cultivation. The Soviets entered the war after repeated requests from the besieged Kabul government. By 1988, Moscow sought to withdraw its troops and called for a nonsocialist, multiparty, coalition government that included a major role for the rebels.

The United States intervened in Afghanistan on the side of ousted feudal lords, reactionary tribal chieftains, and opium traffickers. If this was a worthy cause, what could be an unworthy one? One of the most vicious of the mujahideen leaders was Gulbaddin Hekmatyar, who invaded Afghanistan in 1975 with a force largely created by the Pakistani military and the CIA. A major recipient of U.S. military assistance, he was Afghanistan's prime heroin trafficker. By the mid-1980s, the Afghan mujahideen were providing about half the heroin consumed in the United States and were the world's biggest exporters of opium.

Independent investigators like Steven Galster and John Fullerton, in their respective books on the Afghan war, report that the mujahideen indulged in widespread torture and execution of prisoners, killing of civilians, looting, and raping. These atrocities went unnoticed in the U.S. press.

The Soviets withdrew from Afghanistan in 1988. The Kabul government lasted until 1992, when it was forced from power by the rebels. The triumphant mujahideen immediately began waging war on each other, laying waste to cities, terrorizing civilian populations, and staging mass executions. Hundreds of fundamentalists from other countries like Algeria were trained by the CIA and fought in Afghanistan. After the war, they returned home to carry on organized terrorist attacks against women's-rights activists and other "westernizers" in their own countries.

U.S. intervention in Afghanistan proved not much different from U.S. intervention in Cambodia, Angola, Mozambique, Ethiopia, Nicaragua, and elsewhere. It had the same intent of preventing egalitarian social change, and the same effect of overthrowing an economically reformist government. In all these instances, the intervention brought retrograde elements into ascendence, left the economy in ruins, and pitilessly laid waste to hundreds of thousands of lives.

Famine Relief for Conoco

Just days before he left office in January 1993, President Bush sent troops to Somalia supposedly to safeguard food distribution to its hungry people. Here seemed to be another worthy humanitarian cause. But why would Bush, who spent an entire career in public office untroubled by poverty and hunger at home and abroad, suddenly be so moved to fight famine in Somalia? Why not any of the other African countries in which famine raged? And why such an elaborate military undertaking for humanitarian "famine relief"?

The truth slipped out when the *Los Angeles Times* (January 18, 1993) reported that "Four major U.S. oil companies are quietly sitting on a prospective fortune in exclusive concessions to explore and exploit tens of millions of acres of the Somali countryside." The story notes that "nearly two-thirds of Somalia" was allocated to "the

American oil giants Conoco, Amoco, Chevron and Phillips in the final years before Somalia's pro-U.S. President Mohamed Siad Barre was overthrown." The companies are "well positioned to pursue Somalia's most promising potential oil reserve the moment the nation is pacified." The article reports that "aid experts, veteran East Africa analysts, and several prominent Somalis" believed that "President Bush, a former Texas oilman, was moved to act in Somalia, at least in part," to protect corporate oil's investments there.

Government officials and oil industry representatives insisted there was no link. Still, Conoco (owned by Du Pont), actively cooperated in the military operation by permitting its Mogadishu offices to be transformed into a U.S. embassy and military headquarters. The U.S. government actually *rented* the offices from Conoco. So U.S. taxpayers were paying for the troops in Somalia to protect Conoco's interests, and they were paying the corporation for the privilege of doing so. The *Times* article continues:

> [T]he close relationship between Conoco and the U.S. intervention force has left many Somalis and foreign development experts deeply troubled by the blurry line between the U.S. government and the large oil company. . . . "It's left everyone thinking the big question here isn't famine relief but oil—whether the oil concessions granted under Siad Barre will be transferred if and when peace is restored," [one expert on Somalia] said. "It's potentially worth billions of dollars, and believe me, that's what the whole game is starting to look like."

The story reports that geologists, petroleum experts, and Bush himself, when he was vice president, had publicly noted the region's rich reserves. "But since the U.S. intervention began, neither the Bush Administration nor any of the oil companies . . . have commented publicly on Somalia's potential for oil and natural gas production." Perhaps they became so preoccupied with the humanitarian aspects of the mission that they just honestly forgot about the billion-dollar oil concessions. More likely, they preferred not to alert the public to the possibility that once again American troops were providing muscle for big business.

The rest of the mainstream press (including the *Los Angeles Times* itself, after that one article) remained as reticent about the oil concessions as the Bush and Clinton administrations and the oil companies. The intervention was treated as a humanitarian undertaking and then as a nation-building operation. U.S. and UN troops fought pitched battles, killing several thousand Somalis, in attempts to hunt down a "warlord" deemed too independent-minded. One did not have to be a Marxist to suspect that Washington's goal was to set up a comprador order, not unlike the deposed Siad Barre regime, that would be serviceable to Western investors.

When eighteen U.S. troops were killed in an action in Somalia, the U.S. public began raising questions about the intervention. Not surprisingly, the Clinton administration did not respond forthrightly with: "We are there to build a client state that will serve foreign investors like Conoco." Once more, commentators concluded that here was yet another U.S. foreign policy effort that was ill-conceived, a case of "good intentions gone awry."

The bulk of the U.S. contingent departed from Somalia but 19,000 UN troops remained to continue the job of constructing a nation-state that would be serviceable for the transnationals. In a number of areas in Somalia where there was no UN presence, the tribal strife subsided and local businesspeople, community leaders, students, and representatives from various factions produced peace accords that have held up. In areas where UN forces remained, factional fighting continued, as the clans competed for UN jobs, contracts, and millions of dollars in payments for various services (Op-ed, *New York Times,* July 6, 1994).

On several occasions UN troops came under fire and took casualties. The UN mission in Somalia was deemed a futile effort even by some of its own leaders, who came to believe that they would do best to go home and let the Somalis settle their own affairs.

Elections Yes! (Depending on Who Wins)

U.S. empire builders will use every means at hand, from assassinations to elections, as the circumstances might dictate. They will promote elections abroad, supervise them, buy them, rig them, or undermine them. The CIA has funded procapitalist candidates in electoral contests in Europe, Africa, Latin America, Southeast Asia, and the Middle East. In 1955, the CIA spent $1 million in Indonesia to back a conservative Muslim party, but the party did poorly, while the communists did well. So the CIA set about to negate the election results by backing an armed coup a few years later that failed and another in 1965 that succeeded, costing an estimated 500,000 to one million lives, in what was the worst bloodletting since the Holocaust.

In 1958, the Eisenhower administration poured money into the National Assembly elections in Laos to secure the victory of conservative candidates and thwart the Pathet Lao, an anticapitalist, anti-imperialist party. But the conservatives did poorly and the Pathet Lao did well. Once again, the CIA set about to negate the election results by turning from ballots to bullets. Using a combination of money and coercion, the agency rounded up Meo (a.k.a. Hmong) tribesmen into a private army, for the purpose of making war against the Pathet Lao. As noted in the previous chapter, the CIA assisted the Meo in getting their opium crop onto the world market, a service that tied the tribes closer to the agency.

When the Meo army proved insufficient against the Pathet Lao, U.S. policymakers began an unpublicized aerial war against Laos in 1969 that continued for years. It included B-52 carpet bombing that destroyed village after village and obliterated every standing structure in the Plain of Jars. The surviving rural population lived in trenches, holes, or caves and farmed only at night. Rice fields were turned into craters, making farming impossible. Tens of thousands of people were slaughtered; many starved. Whole regions of Laos were virtually depopulated.

Vietnam was subjected to an equally vicious war of attrition. In Indochina, the U.S. dropped several times more tons of bombs than were used in all of World War II by all sides. John Quigley reported in his book, *The Ruses for War:* "In the south alone, the bombs dropped by B-52s left an estimated 23 million craters, turning the land into swamp, and denuding nearly half of the south's forests. Thousands of our explosive mines remained in the farmland, so that Vietnamese farmers continued to be killed and maimed by them." In mid-June, 1994, the Vietnamese government announced that three million Vietnamese soldiers and civilians had been killed in the war, four million injured, two million made invalids.

In Nicaragua, it was bullets first then ballots. After battering the Nicaraguan people for the better part of a decade in a Contra war, the U.S. national security state promised them aid and an end to the fighting if they voted the procapitalist anti-Sandinista UNO coalition into power, which they did in 1990. Washington poured millions of dollars into that election, seeing it as a way to undermine the Sandinista revolution.

In Mexico in 1988, the popular left candidate Cuauhtemoc Cárdenas, with a decisive lead in the opinion polls, had the election stolen from him. The government confiscated all the ballots and refused to release the voting results for days. Opposition counters were barred from the tallying. When the results were finally announced, to no one's surprise the government candidate, Carlos Salinas, emerged the anointed victor. Hundreds of thousands of Mexicans marched on the National Palace in Mexico City to protest the usurpation of power. U.S. leaders looked upon the fabricated results with quiet satisfaction, making no call for new elections.

Elections in El Salvador in 1984 and 1989 occurred in an atmosphere of terror and political assassination, without benefit of a secret ballot, an honest count, or participation by Left parties. They were, wrote Mike Zielinski (*CovertAction Quarterly,* Summer 1994), "cooked up for international consumption as a fig leaf for a U.S.-backed military dictatorship." In January 1992, the FMLN liberation guerrilla force signed a peace accord with the government and two years later elections were held with the Left participating for the first time. The U.S.-backed, ultra-rightist ARENA government party won in a campaign marked by manipulation, fraud, intimidation, and violence.

With fifty times more money than the FMLN, ARENA waged a media campaign that played on the fears of a population traumatized by twelve years of war, suggesting that the FMLN would abolish religion and murder the elderly. At least thirty-two FMLN members, mostly candidates and prominent campaign workers, were assassinated during the campaign. Some 300,000 people were denied voter registration cards. Another estimated 320,000 were denied access to the polls even when they showed up with cards, their names having been mysteriously omitted from the voting lists. Meanwhile thousands of deceased, whose names were still on the rolls—including ARENA's late leader Roberto D'Aubuisson and the late president José Napoleón Duarte—miraculously managed to vote.

Election-day bus service was concentrated in zones where ARENA supporters predominated, while voters in FMLN areas were often without means of getting to the polls. Many strong

FMLN areas were subjected to military harassment and intimidation during the voting period. ARENA officials controlled the electoral tribunals and invariably handed down rulings that favored their party, turning away some 74,000 voter applicants who could not meet the exacting documentation required. Reminiscent of Mexico, computer vote tallies were delayed for days and failed to match those arrived at by hand. Technicians from opposition parties were expelled from the central computer room on election night.

Even with all the abuses, the FMLN won 25 percent of the seats. One wonders how the Left would have done in an honest contest. Despite all the fraud and intimidation, El Salvador was declared a "democracy" by U.S. political leaders and media. Similar showcase elections have been held in the Dominican Republic after the U.S. invasion, the Philippines under Marcos, Grenada after the U.S. invasion, and a variety of other countries.

All this is not to imply that controlled elections occur only in Third World countries. Campaigns in the United States itself are characterized by prohibitive requirements for minority-party ballot access, expensive filing fees, short filing times, restrictive voter qualifications, limited media access, huge campaign expenses, and no proportional representation, all of which makes it almost impossible for alternative parties, lacking the support of rich donors, to reach mass audiences.

Sometimes all pretense at democracy is dropped, as in Canada, where a law has been passed requiring that parties must field at least fifty candidates in every federal election, at a filing cost of $50,000 ($1,000 per candidate). Parties that failed to do so are "deregistered." They are not allowed to collect funds during the campaign nor spend money on political activities, even in support of their nominated candidates. And they have to liquidate all their assets and turn any remaining funds over to the government. Under this undemocratic law, the Communist party of Canada, along with three other parties were deregistered.

Operation Facelift

In some rare instances, intimidation and fraud prove insufficient and a reformer actually wins the election. Such was the case in 1990 in Haiti, where a populist priest, Father Jean-Bertrand Aristide, labeled a leftist because he sided with the poor against the rich, won an overwhelming 70 percent vote to become Haiti's first freely elected president. During his brief tenure, Aristide fought against corruption in government and for more efficiency in public services. He tried to double the minimum wage from $2 to $4 a *day*, not an hour. He attempted to establish a social security program and land reform projects, all opposed by the banks and the U.S. embassy. Cooperative farms started by peasants in the countryside proved successful until the military repressed them and killed their organizers.

Nine months of democratic efforts were too much for Haiti's military leader, U.S.-trained General Raoul Cedras and his army, which seized power and went on to kill several thousand Aristide supporters and beat and torture many others. The military coup won the support of rich Haitians, foreign investors, and the Roman Catholic hierarchy. Under pressure from the Vatican, Father Aristide's Salesian Order expelled him for "incitation to violence, exaltation of class struggle" and because he "destabilized the faithful" (*San Francisco Bay Guardian*, September 21, 1994).

In its ensuing campaign of terror, the military was assisted by Haiti's National Intelligence Service (SIN), described by investigative journalist Dennis Bernstein as "created, trained, supervised, and funded" by the CIA. "Since its inception, SIN has worked as the eyes and ears of the CIA, while forming the inner circle of Haiti's billion-dollar-plus drug trafficking network."

For over three years Washington did next to nothing to restore Aristide to power. The CIA issued a report claiming he was mentally unbalanced. President Clinton eventually imposed economic sanctions on Haiti and in September 1994 invaded and occupied that country with the professed intent of reviving democracy and restoring Aristide to office.

On the first day of the occupation, however, it was announced that American troops were there to cooperate with the Haitian military. General Cedras would remain in office for another month and neither he nor his cohorts would be required to leave the country. Full amnesty was granted to the entire military for a range of horrific crimes. The U.S. also announced that the junta's assets in U.S. banks amounting to millions of dollars looted from the Haitian people would be unfrozen and given to the generals.

Aristide would be allowed to finish the last months of his term— but for a substantial price. He was strongarmed into accepting a World Bank agreement that included a shift of some presidential powers to the conservative Haitian parliament, a massive privatization of the public sector and a cut in public employment by one-half, a reduction of regulations and taxes on U.S. corporations investing in Haiti, increased subsidies for exports and private corporations, and a lowering of import duties. World Bank representatives admitted that these measures would hurt the Haitian poor but benefit the "enlightened business investors."

At the same time, Aristide supporters were forbidden to demonstrate. U.S. military intelligence, working closely with Haitian intelligence, prepared to round up popular forces and impose massive detentions if necessary. Former national security adviser James Schlesinger (ABC-TV, September 16, 1994) noted that U.S. forces would have to prevent "the Aristide people from making reprisals." Many of them are poor, he said, and may want to loot the houses of the rich. "We will find it hard, and Aristide will find it hard, to control his people. The risk is we will have looting, rioting, and a large number of deaths with which we will be associated." It was clear that the U.S. was in Haiti to protect the rich from the poor and the military from the people, not the other way around. One would think the people were the economic oppressors and armed killers rather than the victims.

During the occupation, U.S. firms in Haiti continued to fire people who tried to unionize and continued to pay workers ten cents an hour for a ten-hour day. Very little if any of the profits of these companies remains in Haiti to contribute to that country's development. Meanwhile conditions in Haiti go from bad to worse. According to the World Bank itself, the number of Haitians who live in absolute poverty rose from 48 percent in 1976 to 81 percent in 1985, indicating a serious spread of malnutrition, disease, and illiteracy.

While ballyhooed by the White House and the media as a rescue operation for democracy, the purpose of the U.S. intervention in Haiti was no different from interventions in numerous other countries: bolster the existing class system, suppress or marginalize the popular organizations, disempower their leaders, and engage in a mild facelift of the military and police, getting rid of some of the more notorious ones while keeping the whole repressive system intact. The interventionist force or its U.N. counterpart will remain in Haiti a long time to carry out what another former national security adviser, Brent Scowcroft, called "complicated pacification" and "hazardous nation-building." In 1915, the last time U.S. troops invaded Haiti, it was under the pretext of "restoring stability." They engaged in a "pacification" program that killed 15,000 Haitians. They did not depart until 1934, after setting up an autocratic military apparatus that has remained in place to this day.

Coming Out of the Capitalist Closet

To summarize the main points I have made about empire: Imperialism is a system in which financial elites forcibly expropriate the land, labor, resources, and markets of overseas populations. The end effect is the enrichment of the few and the impoverishment of the many. Imperialism involves coercive and frequently violent methods of preventing competing economic orders from arising. Resistant governments are punished and compliant ones, or client states, are "rewarded" with military aid.

Attached to no one country, international finance capital is interested in making the world safe for its investments and for the overall system of capital accumulation. Since the end of World War II, the responsibility for doing this has been shouldered preeminently by the United States, at an enormous cost to the American people.

If these assertions are untrue, what is the evidence to support an alternative view? Why has the United States never supported social revolutionary forces against right-wing governments? Why does it harp on the absence of Western democratic forms in certain anticapitalist countries while ignoring brutal and widespread human rights violations in procapitalist countries? Why has it aided dozens of procapitalist military autocracies around the world and assisted their campaigns to repress popular organizations within their own countries? Why has the United States overthrown more than a dozen democratically elected, reformist governments and an almost equal number of left-populist regimes that were making modest moves on behalf of the poor and against the prerogatives of corporate investors? Why did it do these things before there ever was a Soviet Union? And why does it continue to do these things when there no longer is a Soviet Union? Why has it supported and collaborated with narcotic traffickers from Asia to Central America, while voicing indignation about imagined drug dealings in Cuba? Why has it shown hostility toward every anticapitalist party or government, including those that play by the democratic rules and have persistently sought friendly diplomatic and economic relations with the United States? Neither "foolishness" nor a "misguided zeal" nor a need to defend us from "foreign invaders" explains such an unholy consistency.

At a meeting of the National Lawyers Guild in Washington, D.C., May 24, 1987, I heard Edgar Chamorro relate how, when recruited to form a political front for the CIA-backed Nicaraguan Contras, he was told by his CIA advisers that in his public pronouncements he should not mention his desire to restore private property to the owning class of Nicaragua, specifically the land that had been confiscated by the revolutionary Sandinista government and given to poor farmers. Instead he should say he just wanted to put the revolution on the right track toward democracy. His CIA advisers found nothing wrong with his desire to reestablish the privileges of the owning class; indeed, that was what the counterrevolution was all about. They just did not want Chamorro saying it in public, a cautionary approach that revealed not their lack of class consciousness but their keen sense of it.

We should pay less attention to what U.S. policymakers profess as their motives—for anyone can avouch dedication to noble causes—and give more attention to what they actually do. On most occasions they take care not to inform the American people of their real intentions. If this is what some people call a "conspiracy theory," then so be it. In fact, policymakers themselves admit their secretiveness. They regularly emphasize the necessity of operating in secrecy, of keeping both the public and Congress uninformed.

Occasionally, however, policymakers come close to uttering the truth. In 1947, presidential aide Clark Clifford justified intervention in Greece and Turkey by noting that "the disappearance of free enterprise in other nations would threaten our economy and our democracy." In his 1953 State of the Union message President Eisenhower observed, "A serious and explicit purpose of our foreign policy [is] the encouragement of a hospitable climate for investment in foreign nations." In 1982, Vice President Bush said, "We want to maintain a favorable climate for foreign investment in the Caribbean region, not merely to protect the existing U.S. investment there, but to encourage new investment opportunities in stable, democratic, free-market-oriented countries close to our shores."

Even some officers in the U.S. military know who they are working for. At the request of his commanding officer, John Quigley (who later became a critic of U.S. policy) instructed his Marine Corps unit about world affairs:

> When I lectured on Vietnam, few of the Marines knew where it was, or what connection the United States had to it. . . . One Marine [said], "I don't think we need to get in there; there's no reason to get into a war." I explained patiently that there was oil under Vietnam's continental shelf, that Vietnam's large population was an important market for our products, and that Vietnam commanded the sea route from the Middle East to the Far East.

Marine Quigley left out the most important reason. Aside from the oil, the markets, and the imaginary sea-route threat, Vietnam could not be allowed to pursue an anticapitalist revolution that would create an economic system at variance with the one that the U.S. policymakers were dedicated to preserving. If Vietnam was allowed to leave the global free-market orbit, then what of Laos, Cambodia, all of Southeast Asia, and other places around the world?

During the 1992 televised presidential debates, Ross Perot noted that our efforts abroad should be devoted to "defending democracy and capitalism." Sharing the stage was candidate Bill Clinton, who visibly started at Perot's words. Obviously, the outspoken Texas billionaire did not realize that one should not come out so explicitly for *capitalism*. It is a rare occasion when a national leader actually utters the word. For decades, officials and media commentators practiced the utmost discretion regarding that issue, telling us that the Cold War was a contest between freedom and communism, with scant references to the interests of global capitalism.

Still, the times are changing. With the overthrow of communism in Eastern Europe, U.S. leaders and news media began intimating that there was something more than just free elections on their agenda for the former "captive nations." Of what use was political democracy, they seemed to be saying, if it allowed the retention of an economy that was socialistic or even social democratic? Going further, they suggested that a country could not be truly democratic if it were still socialist. They publicly began to acknowledge that a goal of U.S. policy was to install capitalism in the former communist nations, even if those nations had already adopted Western democratic political systems.

The propaganda task of U.S. leaders and opinionmakers was to couple capitalism with democracy, sometimes even treating them as one and the same thing. Of course, they would ignore the many undemocratic capitalist regimes from Guatemala to Indonesia to Zaire. But "capitalism" still sounded, well, too capitalistic. The preferred terms were "free market," "market economy," and "market reforms," concepts that appeared to include more of us than just the *Fortune* 500.

Once elected, Clinton himself began to link democracy and free markets. In a speech before the United Nations (September 27, 1993), he said: "Our overriding purpose is to expand and strengthen the world's community of market-based democracies." In a similar vein, the *New York Times* (October 5, 1993) hailed President Boris

Yeltsin of Russia as "the best hope for democracy and a market economy in Russia." This praise came at a time when Yeltsin was using the army to abolish the constitution and parliament, killing and jailing large numbers of protestors and opponents. It was clear that Yeltsin's dedication to private-profit ownership took precedence over his commitment to democracy, which is why U.S. leaders and media boosted him so enthusiastically. As demonstrated in Russia and numerous other countries, when forced with a choice between democracy without capitalism or capitalism without democracy, Western elites unhesitatingly embrace the latter.

Another example of how the supporters of capitalism are coming out of the closet: In 1994 I wrote a letter to Representative Lee Hamilton, chair of the House Foreign Affairs Committee, urging a normalization of relations with Cuba. He wrote back that U.S. policy toward Cuba should be "updated" in order to be more effective, and that "we must put Cuba in contact with the ideas and practice of democracy . . . and the economic benefits of a free market system." The embargo was put in place to "promote democratic change in Cuba and retaliate for the large-scale seizure of American assets by the Castro regime."

Needless to say, Hamilton did not explain why his own government—which had supported a prerevolutionary right-wing dictatorship in Cuba for generations—was now so insistent on installing democracy on the island. The revealing thing in his letter was his acknowledgment that U.S. policy was dedicated to advancing the cause of the "free market system" and retaliating for the "large-scale seizure of American assets." In so many words, he was letting us know that a fundamental commitment of U.S. policy was to make the world safe for corporate investment abroad.

Those who remain skeptical that U.S. policymakers are consciously dedicated to the propagation of capitalism should note how they now explicitly demand "free market reforms" in one country after another. We no longer have to impute such intentions to them. Almost all their actions and, with increasing frequency, their own words testify to what they have been doing.

CHAPTER 8

DEMOCRATIC GOVERNANCE
VS. THE STATE

We might best think of the American polity as a dual system. First, there are the elections, political personalities, public pronouncements, image engineering, and that handful of visible issues that bestir public officials and win passing attention in the media. This system is taught in the schools, dissected by academics and gossiped about by news pundits.

Then there is the system of coercive state power that is used to protect the dominant structure of the political economy, specifically, the domestic and international interests of finance capital. This system is not taught in the schools nor discussed in the press. Mainstream media commentators seem never to have heard of it. A right-wing commentator like William Buckley *has* heard of it and is part of it, but he would rather that we not think about it. His failure to mention this system of state power is symptomatic of a keen class consciousness rather than a lack of it. To the extent that conservatives like Buckley address class issues, it is to bemoan the excessive privileges and powers wielded by welfare mothers, the unemployed, and advocates of affirmative action.

This dual system roughly reflects the differences between government and state. The *government* deals with visible officeholders, pressure group politics, special interests, and popular demands. It provides the cloak of representative government and whatever substance of democratic rule that has been won through generations of mass struggle.

The *state* has little if anything to do with popular rule or the creation of public policy. It is the ultimate coercive instrument of class power. Frederick Engels noted that in late horticultural society, when substantial surpluses had accumulated, the armed bands of retainers hired by owners to protect their holdings constituted the first embryonic state. Max Weber observed that the state's essential trait, its irreducible feature, is its monopoly over the legitimate uses of force ("legitimate" in that they are legally sanctioned by the constituted authority).

The State Against Democracy

To fulfill its role as protector of existing order, the state often circumvents whatever democratic restraints exist within government. The late FBI chief J. Edgar Hoover noted in a 1970 interview that "justice is merely incidental to law and order. It's a part of law and order but not the whole of it." Indeed, the whole of it, the indispensable goal of the law enforcement agencies of the state, Mr. Hoover made clear by his actions on many occasions, was the preservation of existing class relations, safeguarding the socio-economic structure from fundamental reform and revolutionary change. The preservation of public safety and justice are secondary concerns of the state. The state will violate both when it is deemed necessary to secure the dominant social order.

Lest this be seen as a peculiarly Marxist notion, recall that the English political philosopher John Locke wrote in 1689: "The great and chief end of Men's uniting into Commonwealths and putting themselves under Government, is the Preservation of their Property." And Adam Smith wrote in 1776: "The necessity of civil government grows up with the acquisition of valuable property." And "till there be property there can be no government, the very end of which is to secure wealth, and to defend the rich from the poor." It should be remembered that, from ancient Athens to the present day, the historic purpose of *democratic* government has been just the reverse, to protect the poor from the rich.

Roughly speaking, the difference between government and state is the difference between the city council and the police, between Congress and the CIA. The government mediates public policy. The state orchestrates coercion and control, both overtly and covertly. However, this is a conceptual distinction between what are really empirically overlapping phenomena. The overlap is especially evident in regard to the executive, which is both the center of government policy and the purveyor of state power. The line between state and government also blurs with the courts and certain administrative agencies, and with those members of Congress who serve on committees that deal with intelligence and military affairs and who act primarily as national-security collaborators rather than independent legislators exercising critical oversight.

The conceptual distinction between state and government allows us to understand something about the relationship between politico-economic power and popular governance. For one thing, we become more aware that taking office in government seldom guarantees full access to the instruments of state power. When Salvador Allende, a Popular Unity candidate dedicated to democratic reforms on behalf of the laboring classes, was elected president of Chile in 1971, he took over the reins of government and was able to initiate certain policy changes—such as getting a daily half-liter of milk to every poor child in Chile. But he could never gain control of the state apparatus, the military, the police, the security forces, the intelligence services, the courts, and the fundamental organic law that rigged the whole system in favor of the wealthy propertied class. When Allende began to advance into redistributive politics and against class privilege, the military seized power and murdered him and thousands of his supporters. The CIA-backed, procapitalist state destroyed not only Allende's government but the democracy that produced it.

In Nicaragua, after the left revolutionary Sandinistas lost the 1990 election to a right-centrist coalition, the army and police remained in their hands. However, in contrast to the Chilean military, which was backed by the immense power of the United States, the Nicaraguan military was the *target* of that power and was unable to keep the government on its revolutionary course. At the same time, the anomaly of a left military did sufficiently diffuse state power as to make it difficult for the newly installed Chamorro government to effect the procapitalist changes at a speed pleasing to Washington.

Countries with ostensibly democratic governments often manifest a markedly undemocratic state power. In the United States, not just conservatives but Cold War liberals have used the FBI to protect the security interests of the state. They thereby helped create an independent, unaccountable political police that increasingly involved itself in a variety of unconstitutional actions, including the surveillance of lawful dissidents and protestors. In 1947, President Harry Truman created the Central Intelligence Agency to gather and coordinate foreign intelligence. As ex-senator George McGovern noted (*Parade,* August 9, 1987):

> Almost from the beginning, the CIA engaged not only in
> the collection of intelligence information, but also in covert

operations which involved rigging elections and manipulating labor unions abroad, carrying on paramilitary operations, overturning governments, assassinating foreign officials, protecting former Nazis and lying to Congress.

In a book about J. Edgar Hoover, Anthony Summers noted that the FBI retained close links with organized crime. Former CIA operative Robert Morrow in his book *Firsthand Knowledge* records how unsettling it was to discover that the CIA was cozy with the mob. Over the years, several congressional investigative committees uncovered links between the CIA and the narcotics trade. With its deep operations, laundering of funds, drug trafficking, and often illegal use of violence, the national security state stands close to organized crime. And with its assassinations, intimidation of labor, expropriation of wealth, and influence in high places, organized crime stands close to the state.

Perhaps it should come as no surprise that the USA's most famous mobster, Al Capone, when reflecting on the wider political universe (*Liberty Magazine*, 1929), sounded unnervingly like J. Edgar Hoover:

> The American system of ours, call it Americanism, call it capitalism, call it what you like, gives each and every one of us a great opportunity if we only seize it with both hands and make the most of it. . . . Bolshevism is knocking at our gates. We can't afford to let it in. We have got to organize ourselves against it, and put our shoulders together and hold fast. We must keep America whole and safe and unspoiled. We must keep the worker away from Red literature and Red ruses; we must see that his mind remains healthy.

In other "Western democracies" secret paramilitary forces of neo-fascist persuasion (the most widely publicized being Operation

Gladio in Italy) were created by NATO, to act as resistance forces should anticapitalist revolutionaries take over their countries. Short of that, these secret units were involved in terrorist attacks against the Left. They helped prop up a fascist regime in Portugal, participated in the Turkish military coups of 1971 and 1980, and the 1967 coup in Greece. They drew up plans to assassinate social democratic leaders in Germany, and stage "preemptive" attacks against socialist and communist organizations in Greece and Italy. They formed secret communication networks and drew up detention lists of political opponents to be rounded up in various countries.

Ben Lowe notes (*Guardian*, December 5, 1990), "The operations flowed from NATO's unwillingness to distinguish between a Soviet invasion and a victory at the polls by local communist parties." As far as NATO was concerned there was not much distinction between losing Europe to Soviet tanks or to peaceful ballots. Indeed, the latter prospect seemed more likely. The Soviet tanks could not roll without risking a nuclear conflagration but the anticapitalists might take over whole countries without firing a shot—through the electoral process.

One is reminded of Secretary of State Henry Kissinger's comment, supporting the overthrow of Chilean democracy: "I don't see why we need to stand by and watch a country go communist because of the irresponsibility of its own people." The function of these secret operations was to make sure that the Western democracies did not move in an "irresponsible," anticapitalist direction.

In the United States, various right-wing groups, with well-armed paramilitary camps and secret armies flourish unmolested by the Justice Department, which does not find them in violation of any law. Were they anticapitalist armed groups, they would likely be attacked by federal and local police and their members killed, as happened to the Black Panther party in various parts of the country in the late 1960s and early 1970s.

Conservative Consistencies

The framers of the U.S. Constitution repeatedly asserted in their private talks and letters to one another that an essential purpose of government was to resist the leveling tendencies of the masses and secure the interests of affluent property holders against the competing demands of small farmers, artisans, and debtors. They wanted a stronger state in order to defend the haves from the have-nots.

Today, conservative theorists represent themselves as favoring laissez-faire policies; the less government the better. In practice, however, the "free market" system is rooted in state power. Every corporation in America is publicly chartered, made a legal entity by the state, with ownership rights and privileges protected by the laws, courts, police, and army. If public authority did not exist, there would be no legally established private corporations.

It is ironic that those conservative interests—so overweeningly dependent on government grants, tax credits, land giveaways, price supports, and an array of other public subsidies—keep denouncing the baneful intrusions of government. However, there is an unspoken consistency to it, for when conservatives say they want less government, they are referring to human services, environmental regulations, consumer protections, and occupational safety, the kind of things that might cut into business profits. These include all forms of public assistance that potentially preempt private markets and provide alternative sources of income to working people, leaving them less inclined to work for still lower wages.

While conservative elites want less *government* control, they usually want more *state* power to limit the egalitarian effects of democracy. Conservatives, and some who call themselves liberals, want strong, intrusive state action to maintain the politico-economic status quo. They prefer a state that restricts access to information about its own activities, taps telephones, jails revolutionaries and reformers on trumped-up charges, harasses dissidents, and acts punitively not toward the abusers of power but toward their victims. Conservatives also support repressive crime bills; limitations on the rights of women, minorities, gays and lesbians; censorship of films, art, literature, and television.

For all their complaints about "cultural elites" and "liberal media," right-wingers worked hard to abolish the fairness doctrine, which mandated that persons attacked in the broadcast media had to be given air time to respond. Conservatives, including some in the Democratic party like President Clinton, have supported government subsidies to business and an expansion of the national security establishment.

Conservative propaganda that is intended for mass consumption implicitly distinguishes between government and state. It invites people to see government as their biggest problem. At the same time, such propaganda encourages an uncritical public admiration for the state, its flag and other symbols, and the visible instruments of its power such as the armed forces.

An Executive State

The executive, be it monarch, prime minister, or president, usually stands closer to state functions than the legislature. Some European systems have a prime minister, who deals with legislative and budgetary agendas and related issues, and a president, who is commander in chief of the armed forces and head of state—a duality that gives unspoken embodiment to the distinction between government and state. In the U.S. system, the executive combines the functions both of prime minister and president, of state and government, of popular leader and constitutional monarch.

Marx grasped the special role of the executive in the maintenance of class supremacy. He is often misquoted as having said that the state is the executive committee of the bourgeoisie. Actually, in *The*

Communist Manifesto, he and Engels say that "the executive of the modern State is but a committee for managing the common affairs of the whole bourgeoisie." Thus Marx and Engels recognize the particular class function of the executive. They also implicitly acknowledge that bourgeois government is not a solid unit. Parts of it can become an arena of struggle.

This is true even within the executive branch itself. Thus, the Department of Health and Human Services and the Department of Housing and Urban Development sometimes deal with constituencies and interests that differ markedly from those of the executive as represented by the Pentagon, the Department of Defense, or the Departments of Treasury and Commerce. It is up to the president to resolve these pluralistic interests, making sure that the state remains essentially undiminished.

Nesting within the executive is that most virulent purveyor of state power: the national security state, an informal configuration of military and intelligence agencies, of which the CIA is a key unit.[1] The president operates effectively as head of the national security state as long as he stays within the parameters of its primary dedication—which is the maximization of power on behalf of corporate interests and capitalist global hegemony. If a progressive such as Jesse Jackson were elected president, he would have a hard time getting control of the state, assuming he would be allowed to survive in office.

In 1977, President Carter tried to appoint Theodore Sorenson as director of the CIA. Sorenson, a high-profile liberal, had been a conscientious objector and had filed affidavits defending Daniel Ellsberg and Anthony Russo for their role in releasing the Pentagon Papers. Conservative Republicans on the Senate Select Committee on Intelligence, along with Democrats like chairperson Daniel

---

1. For a more detailed definition of the national security state, see Chapter 2.

Inouye, opposed Sorenson. They said his association with a law firm that dealt with countries in which the CIA had a great deal of influence might cause a "conflict of interest." They questioned his use of classified documents when writing a book and raised a number of other rather unconvincing complaints.

As reported in the *New York Times* (January 18, 1977), "Congressional sources close to the committee suggested that behind such objections lay the conviction on the part of several senators that the CIA director should be a more hardline conservative figure than Mr. Sorenson." Officials in the CIA itself quietly made known their opposition and Sorenson withdrew himself from consideration.

After John Kennedy assumed office in 1961, CIA director Allen Dulles regularly withheld information from the White House regarding various covert operations. When Kennedy replaced Dulles with John McCone, the agency began to withhold information from McCone, its own director. Placed at the head of the CIA in order to help control it, McCone was never able to penetrate to the deeper operations of the agency.

A president who works closely with the national security state usually can operate outside the laws of democratic governance with impunity. Thus President Reagan violated several provisions of the Arms Export Control Act, including one requiring that he report to Congress when major military equipment is transferred to another country. He violated the Constitution by engaging in a war against Grenada without congressional approval. He violated the Constitution when he refused to spend monies allocated by Congress for various human services.

Reagan and other members of his administration refused to hand over information when specific actions of theirs were investigated by Congress. By presidential order, he removed Congress's restrictions on the CIA's surveillance of domestic organizations and activities, even though a presidential order does not supercede an act of Congress. His intervention against Nicaragua was ruled by the World Court, in a 13 to 1 decision, to be a violation of international law, but Congress did nothing to call him to account. He was up to his ears in the Iran-Contra conspiracy but was never called before any investigative committee while in office.

Exposé as Cover-Up

With enough agitation and publicity, government sometimes is able to put the state under public scrutiny and rein it in—a bit. During the late seventies, House and Senate committees investigated some of the CIA's unsavory operations. Congress laid down restrictive guidelines for the FBI, investigated the skulduggery of the Iran-Contra conspiracy, and conducted other important inquiries that proved limited in scope and impact. What remained unquestioned throughout all these exposures are the policy premises and class dedications of the national security state itself.

The Iran-Contra hearings reveal the damage-control function of most official inquiries. As representatives of popular sovereignty, the Joint Select Committee of Congress investigating the conspiracy had to reassure the public that these unlawful, unconstitutional doings would be exposed and punished. However, such exposure conflicted with the first rule of the state, which is that democracy should never do anything to destabilize the state itself.

The process of legitimation through rectification is a two-edged sword. It must go far enough to demonstrate that the system is self-cleansing, but not so far as to destabilize the executive power itself. So the same congressional investigators who professed a determination to get to the bottom of Iran-Contra were also reminding us that "this country needs a successful presidency," meaning that after the scandals of Watergate and President Nixon's downfall, they had better not uncover too much and risk further damage to executive legitimacy.

In sum, the investigation was both an exposé and a cover-up, unearthing wrongdoing at the subordinate level while leaving President Reagan and Vice President Bush largely untouched. In both the coverup and the exposé the purpose was the same: to enhance the legitimacy of the state by a show of self-cleansing, unearthing some of the malfeasance and denying the existence of the rest.

Keeping the Government in Line

Generally, the state is more effective in reining in the government than vice versa. Congressional intelligence committees are usually occupied by members of both parties who identify closely with the needs of the national security state. The Bush administration was reportedly stunned by the appointment of five liberals to the House Intelligence Committee (of twenty or so members). In effect, the administration was saying that the committee has a special relationship to the state and that there should be an ideological test for its members.

Lawmakers who fail the state's ideological test but who occupy key legislative positions run certain risks. When Jim Wright (D-Tex.), became Speaker of the House of Representatives, he began raising critical questions about CIA covert actions against Nicaragua. Wright also took a friendly position toward labor, civil rights, the environment, and human services. Here was a prominent leader publicly questioning a major policy of U.S. imperialism—though Wright never called it imperialism, of course. Criticisms of national security state policy from a left or liberal perspective usually are denied exposure in the media. But because the Speaker of the House was not someone who could easily be ignored, his charges received press coverage. Indeed, he was taken seriously enough to be attacked editorially by the *Washington Post* and the *New York Times* for his comments on Nicaragua.

At the time, I began to wonder aloud if Jim Wright would suffer a fatal accident or die suddenly of natural causes. But there is a neater way of getting rid of troublesome officeholders nowadays. The Republican-controlled Justice Department did a thorough background check on Wright and found questionable financial dealings—not too difficult to do because most politicians are ever in need of campaign funds. He allegedly had accepted improper gifts from a Texas developer and a publisher. A seemingly unwritten rule of U.S. politics is that political leaders caught in shady deals can give up office in order to avoid criminal prosecution. Prominent instances of this trade-off were President Richard Nixon and Vice President Spiro Agnew. This is what Wright quickly did.

Next in line to be Speaker was Tom Foley of Washington State, a flaccid Tip O'Neill retread, who could be counted on never to raise troublesome questions about the murky doings of the national security state and the course of U.S. globalism.

Critics of the national security state are a minority within Congress. Generally, congressional leaders are complicit with the state and with their own disempowerment. Most of them go along with the secrecy that enshrouds CIA operations and U.S. foreign policy. Members serving on intelligence committees rarely fulfill their oversight function; they do not ask too many questions about secret operations, dirty tricks, weapons testing, nuclear arms, counterinsurgency, and aid to tyrants. If one questions too much, then questions might be raised about one's loyalty: Why does this member want to know all these secrets? So they allow the state to go largely ungoverned.

During the Iran-Contra hearings, Representative Jack Brooks (D-Tex.), taking his investigative functions seriously, asked Lieutenant

Colonel Oliver North if there was any truth to the story that he had helped draft a secret plan, code-named Rex Alpha 84, to suspend the Constitution and impose martial law in the USA. A stunned expression appeared on North's face and the committee chair, Senator Daniel Inouye, stopped Brooks from pursuing the question, declaring in stern tones "I believe the question touches upon a highly sensitive and classified area. So may I request that you not touch upon that, sir."

Brooks responded that he had read in several newspapers that the National Security Council had developed "a contingency plan in the event of emergency that would suspend the American Constitution, and I was deeply concerned about it." Inouye again cut him off. It was a tense moment. The committee's leadership was inadvertently admitting that it would refrain from asking about a secret, illegal plan, devised by persons within the national security state for a military coup d'état in the United States.

Constitutional Tyranny

The Constitution has provisions that apply directly to state power, for instance, the power to organize and arm the militia and call it forth to "suppress Insurrections." Provision is made for "the erection of Forts, Magazines, Arsenals, dock-Yards and other needful Buildings" and for the maintenance of an army and navy for both national defense and to establish an armed federal presence within potentially insurrectionary states, a power that was to prove most useful to the moneyed barons a century later when the army was used repeatedly to suppress industrial strikes. Today the control of strikes is a task largely carried out by the police and National Guard.

Article I, Section 9, of the Constitution says that the writ of habeas corpus, intended to defend individuals from arbitrary arrest, can be suspended during national emergencies and insurrections. A presidential edict is sufficient for that purpose. In effect, the

Constitution provides for its own suspension on behalf of executive absolutism.

The national security state has largely succeeded in removing much of its activities from democratic oversight. The CIA has a secret budget that is explicitly in violation of Article I, Section 9, which reads in part: "No Money shall be drawn from the Treasury but in Consequence of Appropriations made by Law. And a regular Statement and Account of the Receipts and Expenditures of all public Money shall be published from time to time." There are no published statements of expenditures for the intelligence community, guessed to be between $35 billion and $50 billion a year. Its appropriations are hidden in other parts of the budget and are unknown even to most members of Congress who vote the funds.

Sometimes the state's determination to set itself above and outside the Constitution is not done secretly but quite overtly, as during the Gulf crisis when Secretary of State James Baker stated, "We feel no obligation to go to Congress for a declaration of war," and President Bush announced he would commit troops to combat regardless of whether he got a single supporting vote in Congress. Rather than being censored for such a lawless declaration and for acting as if the army were his personal force, Bush was hailed in the media for his "strong leadership."

One is reminded of Teddy Roosevelt's boast almost a century ago regarding his imperialist intervention in Panama: "I took the Canal Zone and let Congress debate." The danger of the executive is that it executes. It has its hands on the daily levers of command and enforceable action.

The State in Society

Having said that the national security state is removed from the democratic process, I do not wish to imply that it is removed from our lives. In fact, it reaches deeply into various areas of society. Consider organized labor. The AFL-CIO leadership has sponsored organizations like the American Institute for Free Labor Development (AIFLD) in Latin America, along with similar ones in Africa and Asia, dedicated to building collaborationist, anticommunist, procapitalist unions that undermine the more militant leftist ones both at home and abroad.

The national security state exercises an influence over the corporate media. The CIA owns numerous news organizations, publishing houses, and wire services abroad, which produce disinformation that makes its way back to the states. In the United States, the CIA has actively trained local police Red squads in methods of surveillance and infiltration. As noted earlier, the narcotics traffic has been supported in part by elements in the CIA and various local police forces with the inevitable effect, and probably actual intent, of disorganizing and demoralizing the inner-city masses and discouraging any forms of militant community leadership from emerging.

Numerous crime bills have contained "counterterrorist" measures that pose more dangers to our freedom and security than anything terrorists might do. President Reagan proposed a bill that would have made it a felony to give support to terrorists. Since the administration had designated the Salvador guerrillas as terrorists, then anyone doing solidarity work for democratic dissidents and rebels in El Salvador could have been prosecuted for aiding and abetting "terrorism." So the state tries to repress anti-imperialist efforts and defend the empire by repressing democracy itself. (The Democratic-controlled Congress refused to act on the Reagan bill.)

The process of executive usurpation of power is aided by a conservative judiciary. The courts have given the widest latitude to executive statist prerogatives and supported restrictions on dissent, information, and travel in the name of national security.

Executive usurpation is visible in Eastern Europe, where the peoples of former communist nations now are able to savor the draconian joys of the capitalist paradise. The social benefits they once had under state socialism have been abolished, including the guaranteed right to a job, free education to the highest level of one's ability, free medical care, a secure retirement, low-cost housing, and subsidized utilities and transportation. Replacing these things are the free-market blessings of hyperinflation, the collapse of productivity, widespread unemployment, homelessness, prostitution, poverty, hunger, disease, corruption, ethnic warfare, mob rule, and violent crime.

Hardest hit are the more vulnerable segments of society, among whom the mortality rate has more than doubled: elderly pensioners, the disabled, low-income workers, low-income women and children. Anticipating that they would become part of the First World once they embraced capitalism, Eastern Europeans are rapidly being reduced to Third World misery. A bitter joke circulating in Russia sums it up: Q. What has capitalism accomplished in one year that socialism could not accomplish in seventy years? A. Make socialism look good.

The social misery of the capitalist paradise has caused an anger and discontent in the former communist nations that has to be contained. The political democracy that had been used to overthrow communism now became something of a hindrance for the draconian free-market measures needed for capitalist restoration. So democracy itself needed to be diluted or circumvented in order that the "democratic reforms"—that is, the transition from socialism to free market—be fully effected.

Not surprisingly the presidents of various Eastern European states have repeatedly chosen state over government, calling for the right to put aside democracy and rule by executive fiat. In Russia, President Boris Yeltsin did just that, using force and violence to tear up the constitution, suppress the democratically elected parliament and provincial councils, monopolize the media, kill over a thousand people and arrest thousands more—all in the name of saving democracy. When capitalism is in crisis, the capitalist state escalates its repression, from attacking the people's standard of living to attacking the democratic rights that might allow them to defend that standard of living.

In addition, the material and political aid that the Soviet Union, Bulgaria, and East Germany gave to Third World liberation struggles is no longer forthcoming. Instead, ex-communist countries now join in imperialist wars, as with Desert Storm in 1991, and U.S.-directed interventions, as in Somalia in 1993, further strengthening the interventionist powers of the most powerful imperialist states.

Conspiracy Theory?

Democracy is not a fixed and finished system but a process of continual struggle and realization. Democratic gains are never absolutely secure. They can be rolled back if the contradictions of capitalism threaten to throw the system into crisis. The essence of capitalism, its raison d'être, is not to build democracy, or help working people, or save the environment, or build homes for the homeless. Its goal is to convert nature into commodities and commodities into capital, to invest and accumulate, transmuting every part of the world into its own image for its own realization.

Some people reject this critique as "conspiracy theory." They do not believe that policymakers may sometimes be lying and may have unspoken agendas in the service of powerful interests. They insist that, unlike the rest of us, the rich and powerful do not act with deliberate intent. By that view, domestic and foreign policies are little more than a series of innocent happenings having nothing to do with the preservation of wealthy interests. Certainly this is the impression officials want to create.

I recall a cartoon of two steers in a meadow. One has an anguished look on its face and is saying, "Good grief, I just found out how they make hamburgers!" The other steer is saying, "Oh, you leftist paranoids with your conspiracy theories." Those who are victimized by the policies of the capitalist state should start recognizing, lest they be turned into hamburger, that the conditions they endure are something more than the result of innocent folly and unintended consequences.

In some quarters, just calling something a "conspiracy theory" is considered sufficient grounds for dismissing it. To be sure, there are conspiracy theories that are without foundation, for instance, the view that the Zionists or Catholics or communists or ecologists or Arab terrorists or blacks or the United Nations are taking over America. Whether a conspiracy theory is to be accepted or rejected depends on the evidence. Those of us who claim that highly placed parties in the capitalist state mobilize immense resources to preserve and advance the interests of the existing class system would like the courtesy of something more than a dismissive smirk about "conspiracy theory."

As noted earlier, some people spurn any suggestion that self-interested human agency and power are involved in state policy. To dismiss as conspiracy fantasy all assertions that elite power is consciously and intelligently exercised is to arrive at the implausible position that there is no self-interested planning, no secrecy, no attempt to deceive the public, no suppression of information, no deliberate victimization, no ruthless policy pursuits, no intentionally unjust or illegal gains. It is as if all elite interests are to be considered principled and perfectly honest, though occasionally confused. That certainly would be a remarkably naive view of political reality.

The alternative is to have a coincidence theory or an innocence theory, which says that things just happen because of unintended happenstance, or a muddling through, with a lack of awareness of what is at stake, of who gets what, when, and how. It maintains that workers, farmers, and most other ordinary people might make concerted attempts to pursue their own interests but not the corporate elites and top financial interests, who own and control so much.

For some unexplained reason we are to assume that the rich and powerful, so well-schooled in business and politics, so at home in the circles of power, are unaware of where their interests lie and that they lift not a competent finger in support of them. Such an innocence theory appears vastly more farfetched than the idea that people with immense wealth and overweening power will resort to every conceivable means to pursue their interests—the state being their most important weapon in this heartless and relentless undertaking.

CHAPTER 9

VOODOO ECONOMICS: THE THIRD WORLDIZATION OF AMERICA

The deceptions perpetrated by our leaders to advance the interests of empire abroad are duplicated at home. In both cases, the goal is to undermine popular sovereignty and maximize the capital accumulation process.

Trickle Down to the Free Market

During the Reagan-Bush years (1981–92) we were the victims of voodoo economics. In the years since, we have been the victims of Clintonomics, a slightly milder variation of the same. "Voodoo economics" is a term that George Bush invented during the primary campaign of 1980 when he was running against Ronald Reagan for the Republican presidential nomination. The phrase dogged him when he served as vice president under Reagan. Determined to put it to rest, he contacted cooperative elements at the various TV networks to see if a tape of him saying "voodoo economics" existed. He was told it did not. So in Houston on February 9, 1982, Vice President Bush publicly asserted, "I didn't say it. Every network has searched for it and none can find it. So I never said it."

To claim something never happened because it was not recorded by the media is itself an unsettling assertion.

As it turned out, Bush was caught lying through his teeth. After his Houston speech made the evening news across the country, NBC-TV found a copy of the tape showing him referring to Reagan's tax and budgetary agenda as "voodoo economics." The network played it alongside Bush's denial—one of those rare instances when the media actually did their job and exposed the shameful dissembling that is regularly practiced in high places.

Voodoo economics is really supply-side economics, a trickle-down ideology that goes something like this: If left to its own devices, the free market will provide prosperity for all who are willing to work. Liberated from the irksome and artifical constraints of government regulations and heavy taxes, private investment will grow, bringing greater productivity, more jobs and income for everyone, and less government. A better life awaits us as citizens and taxpayers when an overgrown federal bureaucracy shrinks dramatically and huge budget deficits disappear.

The supply-side theory presumes that as the corporations accumulate wealth, much of it will trickle down to the general public. (This process is known as "feeding the sparrows through the horses," referring to the way sparrows pick undigested grain bits out of horse droppings.) In addition, there presumably will be an expansion of individual freedom as people enjoy greater discretion in how they spend their money, more of it as private consumers and less as taxpayers.

In keeping with supply-side basics, during his administration, President Clinton repeatedly pointed to the private sector as the great source of future jobs and prosperity. He differed from Reagan and

Bush in that he called for a more active role for government in "jump starting" a lagging economy, but he did almost nothing of substance in that direction.

Conservative Double Standards

As noted earlier, conservatives are for weak or strong government depending on what class interests are being served. In recent years they have cut federal assistance programs that benefit the have-nots and eliminated or weakened numerous government regulations, making corporate institutions less accountable to public authority. The deregulation of banking, for instance, resulted in the savings-and-loan disaster. Underwritten by a federal government that was pledged to pick up the losses, private financiers invested wildly for quick profits. When their ventures collapsed, the taxpayer was left holding the bag. The bankers skimmed the cream and the public will be swallowing the multibillion-dollar losses for decades to come.

While insisting that they want to get government "off our backs," conservative supply-siders do not hesitate to use government to intrude upon our private lives and our most intimate moral choices, be it school prayers, flag worshiping, library censorship, or compulsory pregnancy.

Such "cultural" issues are used to recruit middle Americans around the conservative banner. The right-wing fundraiser Richard Viguerie noted that "the abortion issue is the door through which many people come into conservative politics. . . . Then we lead them to concern about sexual ethics" and the "purportedly decadent morality" fostered by "secular humanism," which is represented to them as "the royal road to socialism and communism." This in turn "points the way to commitments to minimally regulated free enterprise at home and to aggressive foreign and military policies" (*Chicago Tribune*, January 25, 1987).

More recently, on a PBS special (September 11, 1994), William Buckley and a group of other conservative pundits openly discussed the need to use cultural and moral issues to activate people and direct them toward a conservative free-market ideology. Rightist leaders have a conscious and quite rational agenda designed to enlist people in the cause of capitalism.

For conservatives, the keystone of all individual rights is the enjoyment of market rights, the right to make a profit off other people's labor, the right to enjoy the privileged conditions of a favored class. By this view, government is an intrusion when it offers school lunch programs, not when it imposes school prayers; an intrusion when it expands its environmental protections, not when it expands the police and military powers of the state; an intrusion when it tries to redistribute income downward, not when it redistributes upward.

Welfare for the Rich

Conservatives denounce liberals in Congress for their "tax, tax, spend, spend" proclivities, for their allegedly profligate habits of deficit spending. In fact, the wildest deficit spenders in our history have been conservative Republicans. The Nixon and Ford administrations produced record peacetime deficits, only to be surpassed many times over by the Reagan and Bush administrations. In the first five years of the Reagan administration, Congress actually appropriated a total of about $12 billion less in discretionary spending than Reagan requested in his budgets.

Big business is always ready to pocket all the profits and socialize the costs. Thus the toxins that industry creates are called *our* toxic waste problem, not Du Pont's or Exxon's. The big corporations just reap the profits from the production process that creates such poisons, while the taxpayers pick up the disposal costs.

In 1962 Appalachia was referred to as "the shame of the nation" because of its poverty. But Appalachia is a rich region not a poor one. Ask the Mellons, Morgans, and Rockefellers, whose mining companies carved out the coal, made vast fortunes, and turned the land into slag heaps and toxic waste dumps. Only the Appalachians are poor. Yet no one suggested that the mine owners pay for the social costs they left in their wake. The diseconomies of capitalism are treated as the public's responsibility. Corporate America skims the cream and leaves the bill for us to pay, then boasts about how productive and efficient it is and complains about our wasteful government.

If there is too much federal welfare spending, it is the welfare that goes to the rich not the poor. In 1994, the amount of money allocated for Aid to Families with Dependent Children (AFDC), the program that is popularly known as welfare, was about $23 billion, or less than 2 percent of the entire budget. An additional $30 billion was spent on low-income assistance such as school lunches and food stamps, programs that often do not reach all of the needy or those most in need.

In contrast, in any given year the federal government hands out more than $100 billion to big business in price supports, payments in kind, export subsidies and export promotions, subsidized insurance rates, new plants and equipment, marketing services, and irrigation and reclamation programs. Additional billions are spent on loan guarantees and debt-forgiveness, including the recent erasure of most of the megabillion-dollar debt owed by the nuclear industry for uranium enrichment services provided by the government.

Welfare for the rich is the name of the game. Over the years, the federal government has sold or leased to private firms, at fees of 1 to 10 percent of true market value, billions of dollars worth of gold, coal, oil, and mineral reserves, along with grazing and timberlands—all of which are the property of the people of the United States. The government has provided billions of dollars to rescue giant corporations like Chrysler, Lockheed, Continental Illinois, and over $500 billion to bail out savings-and-loan institutions. The government distributes billions in research and development grants, mostly to corporations that are then permitted to keep the patents and market the products for profit. The government develops whole new industries, takes all the risks, absorbs all the costs, then hands the industries over to private companies for private gain—as has been done with aerospace, nuclear energy, electronics, synthetics, space communications, mineral exploration, and computer systems.

The government permits billions in public monies to remain on deposit in banks without collecting interest. It tolerates overcharging by firms with which it does business. It awards highly favorable contracts to large companies along with long-term credits and lowered tax assessments amounting to additional billions each year. And through nonenforcement, it has turned the antitrust laws into a dead letter.

In regard to all this corporate largess, no mainstream commentator asks, "Where are we going to get the money to pay for all these things?" an inevitable question when social programs are proposed. Nor do they seem concerned that the corporate recipients of this largesse will run the risk of having their moral fiber weakened by dependency on government handouts. In sum, the myth of a self-reliant, free-market, trickle-down economy is just that, a myth. In almost every enterprise, government provides business with supports, protections, and opportunities for private gain at public expense.

The Tax Game

Under corporate state capitalism, which is what I have been describing, the ordinary citizen pays twice for most things. First, as a taxpayer who provides all these subsidies and supports, and then as a consumer who buys the high-priced commodities and services. Taxation, like public spending, is used to redistribute wealth in an upward direction. Rulers use the coercive power of government to take substantial sums out of our paychecks and give it to the super-rich and the giant cartels. If we take into account all local, state, and federal taxes as well as Social Security, we find that low- and middle-income people fork over a higher percentage of their earnings than do those in the highest bracket. Even the establishment *Washington Post* (April 14, 1985) admitted: "Taxes on the working poor have skyrocketed while taxes on the well-to-do and profitable corporations have declined dramatically." The *Wall Street Journal* added: "One of the ironies of the federal tax system is its bias against the poor." Far from being an irony, it is a consciously pursued policy of supply-side economics.

One of the great victories of Reaganomics was the abolition of the progressive income tax. When Reagan came into office, the top tax bracket was 70 percent. By the time he left, it had been reduced to 28 percent, the same as that of ordinary working people, a flat tax. Both the factory worker who earns $25,000 and the CEO who runs the factory and makes $2,500,000 pay roughly the same tax rate. The situation is even more inequitable because the CEO enjoys a host of deductions that are not available to the worker.

Regressive taxes (when rich and poor pay not the same rate but the same actual amount) have been increased, such as user fees and Social Security taxes. For all his talk about having the rich pay a fairer share of taxes, President Clinton merely lifted the top-bracket tax a few percentage points, kept almost all the privileged write-offs, and proposed a number of regressive excise taxes.

The heavily regressive nature of the Social Security tax has recently made Social Security popular among conservative leaders.

When Reagan first came into office, he held to the right-wing belief that Social Security should be eliminated. Conservatives circulated the false claim that the fund was going bankrupt. Then they realized it actually ran a surplus that was shifted over to general funds and used to pay for FBI agents, nuclear missiles, White House limousines, and other regular budget items. They also realized that the poor pay proportionately more into it than the rich; indeed, most low-income people pay more in Social Security taxes than they do in income tax. So conservatives stopped attacking Social Security and even resisted efforts by some liberals to reduce the tax.

This is not to say that Social Security should be eliminated. But we should reduce the Social Security payroll tax so there is no surplus to be misapplied by the government to purposes other than for what the money was intended. As it now stands, people mistakenly believe their retirement payments are going into a fund that will be waiting for them in their old age. Actually the retirement system is predicated on the assumption that the government's power to tax future wage earners will produce sufficient amounts to finance the pensions of those who are paying exorbitantly high Social Security taxes today.

It has been argued repeatedly by conservatives that, if the wealthy were taxed more heavily, it would not bring an appreciable increase in revenues because there are so few of them. Aside from ignoring the injustice of having the rich pay less, this contention is simply untrue.[1] If corporations and rich individuals were paying taxes today at the 1979 rate, when we still had a 70 percent income tax, the government would be collecting at least $130 billion more per year and there would be far smaller deficits. In 1945, corporations paid 50

---

1. It has been argued that the rich are paying more in taxes today than ten years ago. But that is only because the rich have grown so much richer. The *rate* they pay is far less and the amount they get to keep is proportionately far more than before.

percent of all federal tax revenues. Today they pay 7 percent. The government is borrowing money from the people it should be taxing—a major reason for the huge deficits.

Generous tax breaks are supposed to spur new investments and create new jobs. In fact, firms that are now paying less taxes are also downsizing their work forces. A big tax break is more likely to be turned into a windfall, higher dividend payments to stockholders, and bigger salaries for the top managers. More money is not an inherent incentive to invest if there is insufficient buying power among the working populace.

A Military Feast

Another aspect of voodoo economics is "Pentagon capitalism." Supply-siders give titanic sums to that largest of all bureaucracies within the federal government, the Department of Defense. In eight years Ronald Reagan spent $2.5 trillion on the military, more than was expended in all the years since World War II. Defense production grew 300 percent faster than U.S. industry as a whole. In his four years George Bush budgeted $1.2 trillion for the military. And Clinton is spending money on the military at about the same pace as Bush proposed, the same rate (controlling for inflation) as in 1980, a time of great Cold War tension.

As noted in Chapter 4, military appropriations are a form of government spending pleasing to big business. They offer a potentially limitless, heavily subsidized, low-risk, highly profitable production of commodities. The last four secretaries of defense have pointed out that defense spending creates jobs. So do pornography, prostitution, and narcotics. But there are more socially useful, less wasteful things on which to spend money. In any case, arms spending is so capital intensive that it provides proportionately fewer jobs than any other government expenditure except the space program.

The toll taken by military expenditures on the civilian sector is immense: the neglect of infrastructure maintenance and improvement, the civilian loss of scientific talent to the arms industry, the drastic cuts in human services, and the insolvency of states and cities. What the people of most municipalities spend on armaments in a few weeks (meaning that portion of their federal income taxes that goes to arms) would be enough to wipe out the debts of those municipalities and end their financial crises. In 1992, the $400 million that conservatives proposed cutting from the WIC program, which feeds undernourished infants, children, and pregnant women, is equivalent to what the Pentagon spends in twelve hours. What the federal government spends on consumer protection services all year is equal to what the Pentagon expends in two hours.

A People's National Debt

Another thing the supply-side empire-builders have given us is record deficits and a runaway national debt. The national *deficit* is the money the government spends each year in excess of the revenues it takes in. The national *debt* is the accumulation of yearly deficits. Our national debt consists of money owed by the people of the United States to creditors, usually rich individuals and financial institutions, both American and foreign. When Reagan entered the White House, the national debt was $900 billion. When he left, it was $2.7 trillion, a tripling of the debt in only eight years. Under George Bush's administration the debt rose to $4 trillion, not counting the "off-budget" hundreds of billions for the Savings and Loan bailout. For all his talk about reducing the federal deficit, Clinton's first two budgets offered large deficits and no dramatic reduction in military spending.

As the debt grows in size, it accumulates at an ever greater rate. Since the early 1980s the debt has been growing faster than the gross national income. Every year, a larger chunk of the debt payment is on the interest alone. These interest payments are growing twice as fast as the federal budget itself. By 1994–95, over 80 percent of federal borrowing went to pay for interest on the debt. In other words, as with Third World nations, our national debt is assuming a self-perpetuating structural force of its own, as the government increasingly borrows just to pay the interest on what it previously borrowed.

As more of the federal revenue goes into debt payments, U.S. taxpayers get proportionately less in services. At least 50 cents of every tax dollar goes for servicing the national debt and the military. Over 140 years ago, Karl Marx wrote in *Das Kapital:* "The only part of the so-called national wealth that actually enters into the collective possession of modern peoples is their national debt." Those at the top may take away our timberlands, oil reserves, mineral deposits, pension funds, airwaves, and jobs, but the national debt will always remain safely ours.

Toward 1893

One of the claims made by proponents of voodoo economics is that the federal government will shrink. This has not happened. Another is that state and local governments will be revitalized, performing functions that the federal government had previously pre-empted. This also has not happened. During the late 1980s, state and local governments were among the victims of supply-side economics. The federal government dumped a host of programs upon the states while simultaneously cutting federal transfer payments to them by as much as 40 to 60 percent, causing a major fiscal crisis at state and local levels. This fiscal squeeze brought heartless cutbacks in social services for the most vulnerable portions of the population.

In recent years the top 1 percent of the nation has increased its wealth by over 50 percent while the middle and lower classes lost over $250 billion of wealth (*Los Angeles Times*, January 16, 1994). Government taxing and spending policies are a major cause of this growing gap between rich and poor.

The conservative refrain goes something like this: "If only things were left to the free market and we liberated ourselves from government's meddlesome regulations, then we would see how beautifully a pure capitalism works." In fact, we did practice something close to a pure capitalism in 1893. The result was economic depression and widespread underemployment, nine-year-old children working fourteen-hour days, typhoid and cholera epidemics in Philadelphia and other eastern cities, malnutrition and tuberculosis, and contaminated water and food supplies for the poor. We had uninhibited environmental devastation and horrible work conditions, no pension programs or minimum wage, no occupational or consumer safety regulations, no prohibitions against child labor, and no Social Security, collective bargaining, or industrial unionism. We had unrestrained monopolies and trusts—and enormously high profits. Conditions in the United States in 1893 were not unlike what they are today through much of the Third World.

But for the capitalists of that era, these dismal conditions were not seen as evidence of the system's failure. For them, capitalism in the good old days was working quite well. Success was measured not by the quality of food, drinking water, housing, schools, transportation, and health care, but by the rate of capital accumulation. The function of capitalism then and now has been to invest capital in order to accumulate more capital, and in that sense the system has performed superbly, for those who own and control it.

From the viewpoint of the investor, capitalism is not least but most successful in impoverished Third World countries, where production costs, especially labor costs, are much lower and the value added by labor is several times higher than in the USA. "Value added" is a capitalist term meaning roughly the same as what Marxists mean by "surplus value." It is the value that workers create by their labor in excess of what they are paid. As measured by the value added, the Third World offers more successful forms of capitalism than the social democracies with their strong labor unions, higher wages, and numerous social benefits. Such democratic gains cut into corporate profits and are seen by the capitalists as threatening to the free-market system.

Life conditions under capitalism are most humane in those countries where democratic forces have organized and won some important victories against corporate power, as in the Benelux countries, West Germany, Austria, Sweden, Norway, Canada, and even the United States. Capitalism is most successful in Guatemala, Thailand, Turkey, Nigeria, Indonesia, the Philippines, Paraguay, and other such places where the capital accumulation rate is dramatically higher than in the First World.

Today, the conservative goal is the Third Worldization of America, to reduce the U.S. working populace to a Third World condition, having people work harder and harder for less and less. This includes a return to the "free market," free of environmental regulations, free of consumer protections, minimum wages, occupational safety, and labor unions, a market crowded with underemployed labor, so better to depress wages and widen profit margins. Conservatives also seek the abolition of human services and other forms of public assistance that give people some buffer against free-market forces.

Underemployment is a necessary condition for Third Worldization. Alan Budd, professor of economics at the London Business School candidly observed (*Observer*, June 21, 1992) that the Thatcher government's cuts in public spending were a cover to bash workers: "Raising unemployment was a very desirable way of reducing the strength of the working classes. What was engineered—in Marxist terms—was a crisis in capitalism, which recreated a reserve army of labor, and has allowed the capitalists to make high profits ever since."

With underemployment and poverty come the return of tuberculosis, homelessness, and hunger, and a sharp increase in the number of people who work at nonunion, low-paying, dead-end poverty-level jobs. Real wages have declined at least 10 percent in the last decade.

If that trend continues, will not the economy itself eventually collapse? Certainly, if all wealth accumulates at the top, there will be no one to buy the goods and services produced, and the capital structure itself will severely contract. But there are several things that keep the economy afloat:

First, there is the elevated level of prosperity from which the decline began. Present U.S. consumption is still high by the standards of most nations and by the standards of the 1890s or the Great Depression of the 1930s. The economic decline over the last decade has been dramatic enough, affecting millions of people, yet millions of others are getting by.

Second, there is usually a middle class of sorts in most countries. Even in poor ones, such as India and Brazil, tens of millions are middle class and offer a consumer market.

Third, economic decline is masked somewhat because many working families now have two or three breadwinners to sustain a standard of living that is almost as good as the level provided by one wage earner thirty years ago. Millions of others now hold two or more jobs in order to make ends meet.

Fourth, people are maintaining abnormal consumption levels by borrowing on their future earning power. There exists an enormous consumer debt.

Fifth, the affluent class does its share by increasing its consumption. More money at the top—thanks to tax cuts and fatter profits—means more second and third summer homes, more domestic help, more luxury condos, private airplanes, yachts, high-priced cars, art collections, fabulous vacations, shopping trips abroad, and bigger trust funds for family scions, along with more speculative investments, Treasury bonds, and money market funds.

We are not all in the same boat during hard times. Many people fall overboard and splash about desperately. Others try to stay afloat in leaky skiffs. And still others cruise along in tax-deductible yachts. In 1930, during the depths of the Great Depression, Henry Ford made $30 million and commented that depressions were not all that bad. In the last quarter of 1991, a year designated as the worst recession year since 1939, dividend payments to stockholders hit a record high, causing the president to announce that the economy was doing fine. In fact, the corporate economy *was* doing fine; only the ordinary people were suffering.

From 1980 to the early 1990s, there was a continual shift from production capital to finance capital. The record gains in the stock market were largely gains in speculative investment. Some people would balk at this image of a parasitic class, arguing that corporate investments providentially create new jobs. But according to a report by Working Assets Money Fund (Winter 1991), the number of new stateside jobs created by the *Fortune* 500 between 1980 and 1990, after deducting the cutbacks and layoffs, was zero.

Old Problems, No Solutions

Textbook Keynesianism says that government can act as a countervailing force to mitigate the effects of the boom-and-bust business cycle, leveling off the hills and filling in the valleys. When the economy is overexpanding and inflation looms, the government serves as a brake. It raises taxes to cut down on buying power. It raises interest rates to increase the cost of money and slow down borrowing and investment. And it reduces its own spending.

When the economy is going into recession, the government takes the opposite tack. It decreases taxes so that people will have more money to spend. It cuts interest rates to make it easier to borrow and invest. And it augments its own spending in order to expand demand. But when it cuts taxes and increases spending, it produces a deficit. Given the size of the national debt, the government can no longer spend its way out of a recession. The national debt is the financial ozone hole in the political economy. We now have record deficits and record spending without creating much impetus for a more vigorous economy.

Inflation has slowed down since the 1970s, but prices are still climbing, especially for essentials on which the poor spend the bulk of their money. The media have conveniently overlooked this phenomenon. A news report on National Public Radio, April 17, 1989, noted: "If you take food, fuel, and housing out of the equation, inflation has been really quite moderate." To be sure, and if you remove a few other major items, it disappears altogether.

A key reason why the United States is becoming increasingly like the Third World is because corporate America is going Third World, literally, not only downgrading jobs and downsizing, but moving whole industries to Asia, Latin America, and Africa.

The aim of modern imperialism is not to accumulate colonies nor even just to provide outlets for capital investment and access to natural resources. The economist Paul Sweezy noted that the overall purpose is to turn Third World nations into economic appendages of the industrialized countries, encouraging the growth of those kinds of economic activities that complement the advanced capitalist economies and thwarting those kinds that might compete with them.

Perhaps Sweezy relies too much on the nation-state as the unit of analysis. The truth is, the investor class also tries to reduce its *own* population to a client-state status. The aim of imperialism is not a national one but an international class goal, to exploit and concentrate power not only over Guatemalans, Indonesians, and Saudis, but Americans, Canadians, and everyone else.

Presidents and plutocrats always tell us not to be negative about the economy. In 1930, after the economy sank into the Great Depression, and ten million people were thrown out of work, William Crocker, president of the First National Bank of San Francisco, said that conditions compared favorably with those existing before the crash: "People are in an unnecessarily negative frame of mind and have stopped buying things, and this has caused everything to tailspin." President Bush came to the same conclusion about the 1990–91 recession, urging us to go out and do more shopping.

Both Crocker and Bush were reducing economic reality to a subjective psychological condition, thereby reversing cause and effect. Recession is not caused because people suddenly become less inclined to buy. It is the other way around: people buy less because their jobs are abolished or downgraded and they have less buying power. One would think that point is evident enough.

More than 150 years ago Karl Marx predicted that depressions would continue to occur because workers are not paid enough to buy back the goods and services they produce. He knew more about the future than our presidents and plutocrats would have us know about the present.

CHAPTER 10

THE EMPIRE IN ACADEMIA

Within U.S. universities are people who do "risk analysis" to help private corporations make safe investments in the Third World. Others work on consumer responses to marketing techniques, labor unrest, and union busting. Still others devise new methods for controlling rebellious peoples at home and abroad, new weapons delivery systems and technologies for surveillance and counterinsurgency. (Napalm was invented at Harvard.) Whether studying Latin American villagers, inner-city residents, or factory workers, for handsome fees these scholars and scientists offer bright and often ruthless ideas about how to keep the world safe for those who own it.

On these same campuses one can find ROTC programs difficult to justify by any normal academic standard. The campuses also are open to recruiters from various corporations, the CIA, and the armed forces. In 1993, an advertisement appeared in student newspapers across the nation promoting "student programs and career opportunities" with the CIA. Students "could be eligible for a CIA internship and tuition assistance" and would "get hands-on experience" working with CIA "professionals." The advertisement did not explain how full-time students could get "hands-on experience" as undercover agents. Would it be by reporting on professors and fellow students who voiced iconoclastic views?

A Temple of Knowledge

At these same colleges and universities can be found faculty and administrators, including many engaged in the activities described above, who argue with all apparent seriousness that a university is an independent community of neutral scholars, a place apart from the immediate interests of this world, a temple of knowledge. In reality, many universities have direct investments in corporate America in the form of substantial stock portfolios. By purchase and persuasion, our institutions of higher learning are wedded to institutions of higher earning. In this respect, universities differ little from such other social institutions as the media, the arts, the church, schools, and various professions, all of which falsely claim independence from a dominant class perspective.[1]

During the late 1960s, at rallies and teach-ins, many students and some faculty began to educate themselves about the injustices and horrors of a far-off war in Indochina. At first, they questioned only the war, then the leaders who produced it, and then the system that produced the leaders, including that part of the system represented by the actively complicit university. Crossing the line from a liberal complaint to a radical analysis, some campus protestors concluded that the Vietnam War was not a "mistake," but part of a long-standing pattern of U.S. interventionism designed to make the world safe for multinational corporate exploitation. They also came to realize

---

1. For a fuller discussion of this point, see my *Land of Idols: Political Mythology in America* (New York: St. Martin's Press, 1994), Chapter 7, "Monopoly Culture."

that protest was not just a matter of creating a dialogue and persuading supposedly well-intentioned but ill-informed leaders. Rather it entailed increasingly difficult confrontations with the repressive powers of the state and its auxiliary institutions, and with leaders who were not misguided or confused but who knew perfectly well what they were doing.

The university represents itself as a citadel of free thought. There is even a special term, "academic freedom," to describe its favored circumstance. In truth, the system of rule within the average institution of higher learning owes more to Sparta than to Athens. Reflective of the larger society around it, most universities and colleges are more ideological factories than intellectual founts, places where criticisms of imperialism are in scarce supply and where students mortgage their future to capitalism as a social order.

A Matter of Some History

Ideological repression in academia is as old as the nation itself. Through the eighteenth and nineteenth centuries, most colleges were linked to one or another religious faith. They were usually controlled by devout trustees who believed it their duty to ensure faculty acceptance of denominational preachments.

The dogmas of racism also enjoyed a secure place in the educational institutions of that day. In the early 1800s, trustees at Northern colleges prohibited their faculties from engaging in critical discussions of slavery and advocating abolitionism. At southern colleges, there was never a question of advocating abolitionism. Faculty actively devoted much of their intellectual energies to justifying slavery and injecting white supremacist notions into the overall curriculum.

In the 1870s and 1880s, Darwinism was the great taboo subject in U.S. higher education. Presidents of nine prominent eastern colleges went on record as prohibiting the teaching of evolutionary theory. What is called "creationism" today was the only acceptable viewpoint in most of the nation's "free and independent" schools.

By the 1880s, rich businessmen came to dominate the boards of trustees of most universities and colleges (and they continue to do so to this day). They seldom hesitated to impose ideological controls. They fired faculty members who expressed heretical politico-economic ideas on and off campus, attended Populist party conventions, championed antimonopoly views, supported free silver, opposed U.S. imperialism in the Philippines, or defended the rights of labor leaders and socialists. Among those dismissed were such notable scholars as Richard Ely, Edward Bemis, James Allen Smith, Henry Wade Rogers, Thorstein Veblen, E. A. Ross, and Scott Nearing.

The firing of radical or otherwise heretical faculty escalated around World War I. Teachers were let go who expressed doubts about the war or opposed the sale of liberty bonds or advocated internationalism. University officials such as Nicholas Murray Butler, president of Columbia University, explicitly forbade faculty from criticizing the war, arguing that such heresy was no longer tolerable, for in times of war, wrongheadedness was sedition and folly was treason.

A leading historian, Charles Beard, was grilled by the Columbia University trustees, who were concerned that his views might "inculcate disrespect for American institutions." In disgust, Beard resigned from Columbia, declaring that the trustees and Nicholas Murray Butler sought "to drive out or humiliate or terrorize every man who held progressive, liberal, or unconventional views on political matters."

Academia certainly never has been receptive to persons of anticapitalist persuasion. Even during the radical days of the 1930s there were relatively few communists on college teaching staffs, and they usually were assistants, instructors, and others of marginal and insecure status. An open identification with communism was not conducive to career survival.

The repression of campus heterodoxy reached a heightened intensity during the late 1940s and early 1950s with McCarthyism and the witch-hunt investigations conducted at the state and federal levels. Among the faculty driven from the academy were those associated with the Communist party or one of its affiliated organizations, along with others who refused to tell inquisitors whether they or any associates were or had ever been party members. Sociologist Sigmund Diamond was deprived of a position at Harvard by then-dean McGeorge Bundy (who later distinguished himself as one of those bright Washington policymakers who gave us the Vietnam War). Diamond's crime was that he would not name names to the FBI.

Others, like economist Paul Baran at Stanford, had no affiliation with the Communist Party but were Marxists, which was virtually as bad. The rooting out of anticapitalist faculty was done by congressional committees, state legislative committees, and, in many instances, university administrations. Administrators across the land developed an impressively coherent set of practices to carry out their mission of purging faculty rosters.

One prominent Communist party member, Herbert Aptheker, a stimulating teacher and productive historian, was unable to get a regular academic appointment in more than fifty years. In 1976, he was invited to teach a course at Yale University for one semester, but the administration refused to honor the appointment. Only after eighteen months of protests by students and faculty did the Yale oligarchs give in. Even then, precautions were taken to ensure that Aptheker not subvert too many Yalies. His course was limited to fifteen students and situated in the attic of a dingy building at a remote end of the campus. Aptheker had to travel from New York to New

Haven for his once-a-week appearance. He was given no travel funds and was paid the grand sum of $2,000 for the entire semester. Yale survived the presence of a bona fide Communist but not without institutional officals trembling a bit. They were not afraid that Aptheker by himself would undermine the university but that his appointment might be the first step in an opening to anticapitalist viewpoints that had been kept out of Yale for generations.

Thousands of other faculty, never called up before any investigative body, still experienced chilling effects. In a study of academia during the McCarthy period, Paul Lazarsfeld and Wagner Thielens, Jr., reported that a need to prove one's loyalty permeated faculty ranks. Almost any criticism of the existing politico-economic order invited the suspicion that one might be harboring "communist tendencies." Faculty who refused to sign loyalty oaths were dismissed.

Some academics criticized the investigations for destroying morale and "making it more difficult for a free society to ward off the real totalitarian communist menace." Thus, even when denouncing the anticommunist witch hunts, they did so from an anticommunist premise. They argued that too many innocent people were being hounded out of their jobs and silenced in their professions. The implication was that the inquisiton was not wrong, just clumsy and overdone, that it was quite all right to deny Americans their constitutional rights if they were really "guilty," (communists), as long as the careers of "innocent" people (noncommunists) went undamaged.

The Open and Closed University

Faced with student demonstrations, sit-ins, and other disruptions during the Vietnam era, university authorities used the carrot and the stick, a combination of liberalizing and repressive measures. They dropped course-distribution requirements and abolished parietal rules and other paternalistic restrictions on student dormatory life.

Courses in African American studies and women's studies were set up, along with a number of other experimental social science programs. These latter offered community-oriented courses, innovative teaching methods, and a conscious attempt to deal with contemporary issues.

Along with the concessions, university authorities launched a repressive counteroffensive. Student activists were expelled, beaten by police, arrested, drafted into a war they opposed, and—at places like Kent State and Jackson State—shot and killed. Radicalized faculty lost their jobs and some, including myself, were badly beaten by police during campus confrontations.

The repression continued through the 1970s and 1980s. Angela Davis, a Communist, was dismissed by the University of California, Los Angeles. Marlene Dixon, a Marxist-feminist sociologist, was fired from the University of Chicago and then from McGill University for her political activism. Bruce Franklin, a noted Melville scholar, a tenured associate professor at Stanford, author of eleven books and one hundred articles and an outstanding teacher, was fired for "inciting" students to demonstrate. Franklin later received an offer from the University of Colorado that was quashed by its board of regents, who based their decision on a packet of information supplied to them by the FBI. The packet included false rumors, bogus letters, and unfavorable news articles.

At the Unversity of Washington, Seattle, Kenneth Dolbeare's attempts to build a truly pluralistic political science department with a mix of conservative, mainstream, and radical faculty, including women and people of color, came under fire from the administration. After a protracted and demoralizing struggle, Dolbeare left the university. Progressive members of the department, including Albert Black, Allen Polawski, Judy Lamare, and an African American faculty member, Trevor Chandler, were let go. Philip Meranto, the only radical with tenure, eventually quit in disgust. A widely published urban affairs scholar and excellent teacher, Meranto was unable to secure another regular academic appointment. Other progressives on the UW Seattle campus, including noted Chicano scholar Carlos Muñoz, John Chambliss in philosophy, and Jeff Morris in economics were denied reappointment.

Similar purges occurred across the nation. A well-published historian and original scholar, Jesse Lemish, who wrote a critique of the hidden ideological presumptions of mainstream historiography, was fired from the University of Chicago because, as his department chair explained to him, "Your convictions interfered with your scholarship." Also dismissed by the University of Chicago was Staughton Lynd, historian and prominent antiwar activist. The sociologist Paul Nyden, who taught at the University of Pittsburgh and also actively worked with dissidents in the United Mine Workers, was fired for political reasons. He sued and collected out of court. Despite the support of students and faculty, the Marxist sociologist Peter Seybold was denied renewal at the University of Wisconsin, Parkside.

The purges from the 1960s to today are too numerous to record here. Eight of nine antiwar professors who tried to democratize the philosophy department at the University of Vermont were denied contract renewals in swift succession. Within a three-year period in the early seventies, at Dartmouth College, all but one of a dozen progressive faculty who used to lunch together were dismissed. In 1987, four professors at the New England School of Law were fired, despite solid endorsements by their colleagues. All four were involved in the Critical Legal Studies movement, a left-oriented group that views the law as largely an instrument of the corporate rich and powerful. The school's trustees, drawn largely from the corporate rich and powerful, preferred that such ideas not be taught.

To this substantial list I can add my own name. In 1972, at the University of Vermont, I was denied renewal by the board of trustees, despite the support of my students, my entire department, the faculty senate, the council of deans, the provost, and the university president. The board could find no fault with my teaching or long list of publications but decided that my antiwar activities constituted "unprofessional conduct."

In their privately published book, *Guarding the Ivy Tower*, Philip Meranto and Matthew Lippman list over fifty additional cases of faculty across the country who were purged during the 1970s because of their political beliefs and activities. The list was representative rather than exhaustive. One could add many more instances involving political scientists, economists, historians, sociologists, psychologists, and even chemists, physicists, mathematicians, and musicologists.

Whole departments and even whole schools and colleges have been eradicated for taking the road less traveled. At Berkeley, the entire school of criminology was abolished because many of its faculty had developed a class analysis of crime and criminal enforcement. Those among them who taught a more orthodox criminology were given appointments in other departments. The radicals were let go.

In 1970, in response to student demands, an experimental Social Science College was formed at the State University of New York, Buffalo. Within a few years the entire school came under fire from SUNY administrators because two-thirds of its thirty faculty members took a radical approach to their work. Some of their courses used Marxist books and reached over one thousand students, including workers who attended night school. The example of a successful Marxist program that built growing links with the labor movement was too much for university officials. The experimental college was abolished in 1976.

The purging of dissidence within the universities continues to this day. Economist Rob Wright was denied a contract at Napa Valley Community College in May 1994 by a review committee composed of his conservative department chair (who accused Wright of "teaching communism"), the chair's wife (who taught typing), her staff secretary, and the head of the social science division (who had once publicly identified himself as Wright's "personal nemesis"). Another member of the committee, a conservative accountant, told Wright he was appalled at how the committee seemed to have made up its mind about Wright's candidacy before even looking at his credentials. Twenty unsolicited letters by students praising Wright's teaching abilities were mysteriously "misplaced" by the committee and never found.

Lefties Need Not Apply

Even more frequent, but less visible, than the firings are the nonhirings. A faculty member at Boston University told me that there was no possibility of his school hiring anyone known to be politically to the left. Highly qualified social scientists, who were also known progressives, applied for positions at institutions in California, Texas, Illinois, Colorado, New York, and other places too numerous to mention, only to be turned down in favor of candidates who—as measured by their training, publications, and teaching experience—appeared less qualified. The pattern became so pronounced at the University of Texas, Austin, in the mid-1970s, that graduate students staged a protest and charged the university with politically discriminatory hiring practices.

In 1980, when visiting Reed College in Oregon, I observed students circulating a statement complaining about the total absence of faculty who offered critical perspectives. One student said to me: "If we want to read any left alternative critiques, we have to do it on our own in addition to all the regular course work we get. And we seldom get the chance to discuss it in class." When I asked some Reed faculty about this, they admittedly could not recall any colleagues who offered a critical left perspective nor did they seem too concerned about the lack of ideological diversity.

In 1981, the political science department of Virginia Commonwealth University invited me to become chairperson, but they were overruled by the dean. She announced that it was unacceptable to have a leftist as head of a department. It is evident that academia speaks with two voices. One loudly proclaims, "If you are a productive scholar and good teacher, we are likely to have a job for you." The other whispers almost inaudibly, "You must have the correct mainstream ideological paradigm and avoid active dissidence; if not, it really doesn't matter what your scholarly and pedagogical performance is."

Scholars of an anticapitalist, anti-imperialist bent are regularly discriminated against in the distribution of research grants and scholarships. For instance, C. Wright Mills, after writing *The Power Elite*, was abruptly cut off from foundation funding. Dissident scholars are rarely considered for appointments within their professional associations and are regularly passed over for prestigious lecture invitations and appointments to editorial boards of the more influential professional journals.

In the "free and pluralistic" university, faculty think twice about introducing a controversial politico-economic perspective in class. A historian who has extensively studied political repression in academia, Ellen Schrecker, writes that when one young instructor and a group of her colleagues decided to offer "Marxism" as part of a social history course, she was warned by an older faculty member, "an ordinarily calm and rational gentleman," that it would be "unwise for their department to list a course on Marxism in the catalogue."

An instructor at Seton Hill College in Pennsylvania confided to a leftist student that he subscribed to a number of left publications and was well versed in Marxist theory but the administration refused to let him teach it. The student wrote to an associate of mine, "I've had classes with this prof for two years and never suspected." There probably are many such instances of self-censorship among faculty.

On some campuses, administrative officials have been known to monitor classes, question the political content of books and films, and screen the lists of guest speakers. In 1986, the board of regents of the University of Colorado, Boulder, openly debated whether to freeze the funds of the student-run Cultural Events Board. Democratically elected by the student body, the board had invited a few speakers who drew large, enthusiastic audiences, but who were politically offensive to the conservative regents. Under the guise of maintaining academic standards, the regents sought to "upgrade" the quality of speakers with a roster that was more to their ideological taste.

In recent years, despite their protestations about budgetary austerity, university administrations around the country have paid huge sums for one-night appearances to guest lecturers like conservative ideologues William Buckley and George Will, war criminals Henry Kissinger and Alexander Haig, and convicted Watergate felon G. Gordon Liddy.

Those political analysts whose views are beyond the acceptable boundary of capitalist orthodoxy are regularly denied access to the major media. When they do receive mainstream coverage, it is usually of a defamatory kind. Probably the lowest hit I ever received in the press was from the *National Enquirer*, a supermarket tabloid, that ran an article headlined: U.S. PROFESSORS ARE TEACHING OUR STUDENTS AMERICA IS EVIL AND COMMUNISM IS GOOD. It was accompanied by a photograph of me juxtaposed with one of Karl Marx, and a graphic of a hammer and sickle slicing across a map of the United States, with blood dripping from the wound. The article referred to my "twisted teachings" and quoted me: "Capitalism does exploit people here and abroad. The system is mainly for the benefit of the rich at the expense of working people and the middle class." The quotation was accurate enough, but framed in such a way as to appear more like a treasonous utterance than a comment about social relations in the USA.

Elastic Criteria

In recent years, the guardians of academic orthodoxy have learned to operate in a more circumspect fashion. Rather than voicing an open intolerance for radicals, they try to find seemingly professional grounds for rejection. They will say the candidate has not published enough articles. Or if enough, the articles are not in conventionally acceptable academic journals. Or if in acceptable journals, they are still wanting in quality and originality, or show too narrow or too diffuse a development.

Seemingly objective criteria can be applied in endlessly subjective ways. Facing a tenure battle at Tufts University in 1986, the progressive political scientist Robert Elias had his book subjected to fifteen outside reviews, five or six more than the usual number in such evaluation procedures. When all fifteen proved positive, the administration called for an additional five outside reviewers. To Elias, it seemed they were "just looking for a negative review."

John Womack, one of the very few Marxists ever to obtain tenure at an elite university, and who became chair of the history department at Harvard, ascribes his survival to the fact that he was dealing with relatively obscure topics: "Had I been a bright young student in Russian history and taken positions perpendicular to American policy . . . I think my [academic] elders would have thought that I had a second-rate mind. Which is what you say when you disagree with somebody. You can't say, 'I disagree with the person politically.' You say, 'It's clear he has a second-rate mind'" (*Washington Post*, January 1, 1983).

The guardians of orthodoxy also indulge in what might be called "the search for the supreme candidate." When confronted with a highly qualified but politically unacceptable person, they will inquire whether he or she is "the very best in the field." Thus an outspokenly antiwar and anticapitalist activist at the University of Illinois, John Lombardi, a chemist, was denied tenure in 1972 by his conservative chair, a firm supporter of the U.S. war in Vietnam. He wanted to know if Lombardi could claim to be the "number one" spectroscopist in the country. While internationally recognized for his outstanding research in spectroscopy, Lombardi would not make such a claim nor did he know who could.

A similar pretext was used against Bertell Ollman at the University of Maryland when he was offered the chair of the political science department. After accepting the position, Ollman was red-baited by the media and some trustees, who openly opposed having a Marxist as chair. The administration withdrew the offer. Following an extended legal battle, Ollman was denied the position. While the administration could not deny that he was eminently qualified, it professed a commitment to recruiting someone who might be still better, indeed, "the very best." The suggested image was of the greatest scholars in the world (whoever they might be) beating a path to College Park, Maryland, to serve as chair of the political science department.

College administrations are not always naysayers. They can prove quite generous with promotions and tenured appointments when candidates hold the right views—sometimes even when their scholarly output is wanting in quantity or quality. The administration at the University of Vermont brought in someone to chair the philosophy department who, by a 9 to 1 vote, the department had turned down as insufficiently qualified. He proceeded to purge all the nontenured members who had voted against him.

Over the objections of the political science department of the University of Maryland, Baltimore, the chancellor gave tenure to Walter Jones, not a particularly distinguished member of the profession. Jones was then made vice chancellor, from which position he denied tenure to fellow political scientist Phillip Brenner, overruling a unanimous recommendation of the school's promotion and tenure committee. Cleverly enough, Jones faulted Brenner, an expert on Congress and foreign policy, for not being sophisticated and rigorous enough in his Marxism. Had Brenner offered a more explicit Marxist analysis, one wonders if he then would not have been faulted for being doctrinaire and rigid.

Professional criteria prove especially elastic for those emigrés from communist countries who are brought to the United States under the hidden sponsorship of national security agencies and immediately accorded choice university positions without ever meeting normal academic standards. Consider the case of Soviet emigré and concert pianist Vladimir Feltsman, who, after receiving a first-rate, free musical education in the Soviet Union, defected to the United States in 1986—with the help of the U.S. embassy. In short time, Feltsman gave a White House concert, was hailed by President Reagan as a "moral hero," and was set up in a posh Manhattan apartment. He then was appointed to the faculty of the State University at New Paltz, New York, where he taught one course a week for a salary that was twice that of a top-ranking professor. In addition, he was awarded an endowed chair and a distinguished fellowship. All this at New Paltz, a school that was poorly funded, with low salaries, heavy teaching loads, and inadequate services and supplies for students. Perhaps Feltsman was the greatest pianist of all time; more likely, his meteoric rise in academia had something to do with ideological Cold War considerations.

Presumptions of Objectivity

Mainstream academics maintain that their politically orthodox brands of teaching and research are the only ones that qualify as proper scholarship. Such was an argument used to deny Samuel Bowles tenure at Harvard. Since Marxist economics is not really scholarly, Bowles was neither a real scholar nor a genuine economist. (The decision seriously split the economics department and caused Nobel Prize–winner Wassily Leontif to quit Harvard in disgust.) Centrist ideologues seem unaware that this view might itself be an ideological one, a manifestation of their own self-serving, unexamined political biases. Having judged Marxist scholars as incapable of disinterested or "real" scholarship, the centrists can refuse to hire them under the guise of protecting rather than violating academic standards.

Many mainstream academics manifest a remarkable detachment from the urgent realities of the world. What is unsettling is how this is treated as a scholarly virtue. Supposedly such detachment helps them to retain their objectivity. In fact, much of the best scholarship comes from ideologically committed scholars. Thus, it is female and African American researchers who respectively have produced the best work on the oppressions of sexism and racism, areas that their white male colleagues never imagined were fit subjects for study. It is they, in their partisan urgency, who have revealed the unexamined sexist and racist presumptions of conventional scholarship in the sciences and social sciences.

Likewise, it is leftist intellectuals who have produced the best work on popular struggles and often the only revealing work on the political economy of class power, subjects remaining largely untouched by "objective" centrists. Their partisan concerns have inspired some exciting and challenging scholarship. In sum, a dissenting ideology can free us from long established blind spots and awaken us to things overlooked by the established orthodoxy.

In any case, mainstream academics are nowhere nearly as detached as they claim. Their work already is riddled with unexamined values that are treated as empirical truths, while empirical hypotheses introduced by radicals are dismissed as polemics or value judgments. They inject their biases into what they say and leave unsaid and, as already noted, into their decisions regarding recruitment, promotion, tenure, and curriculum. One goal of any teacher should be to introduce students to bodies of information and analysis that have been systematically ignored or suppressed in the press, the academy, and society, a task that usually is better performed by dissident faculty than by those who accept existing institutional and class arrangements as the natural order of things.

Orthodox ideological strictures are applied not only to scholarship but to a teacher's outside political activity. Upon entering an academic profession, one does not forfeit one's rights under the First Amendment nor does one join some totalitarian priesthood. Yet that appears to be the case in regard to dissident political affiliations. Thus, at the University of Wisconsin, Milwaukee, an instructor of political science, Ted Hayes, an anticapitalist, was denied a contract renewal because he was judged to have "outside political commitments" that made it impossible for him to be an objective, balanced teacher. Two of the senior faculty who voted against him were state committeemen of the Republican party in Wisconsin. There was no question as to whether *their* outside political commitments interfered with their objectivity as teachers or with the judgments they made about colleagues.

Evron Kirkpatrick, who served as director of the American Political Science Association for more than twenty-five years, said in a speech in Washington, D.C.: "I have always believed that the knowledge we gain as scholars should provide a basis for others or for ourselves to play an active, effective and sound role in government and politics." He then enumerated the many political scientists who occupied public office, worked in electoral campaigns or served officialdom in various capacities. His remarks evoked no outcry from his mainstream colleagues on behalf of scientific detachment. It seemed there was nothing wrong with political activism as long as one played a "sound role in government" rather than a dissenting role against it. Establishment academics like Kirkpatrick never explain this double standard. Nor do they explain how they are able to avoid injecting politics into their science while so assiduously injecting their science into politics.

How neutral in their writings and teachings were such scholars as Zbigniew Brzezinski, Henry Kissinger, and Daniel Patrick Moynihan? Despite being blatant proponents of American industrial-military policies at home and abroad—or because of it—they enjoyed meteoric academic careers and subsequently were selected to serve as prominent acolytes to the circles of power. Outspoken political advocacy is not a hindrance to one's career as long as one advocates the right things.

Quarantine the Survivors

The relatively few progressive dissidents who manage to get tenure usually discover that their lot is one of isolation within their own departments. They endure numerous slights and are seldom consulted about policy matters. They are not likely to be appointed to committees dealing with curriculum, hiring, and tenure, even when such assignments would be a normal part of their responsibilities.

At the University of Washington, Philip Meranto, a tenured anticapitalist political scientist and noted activist, was frozen out of all departmental decisions and department social life. Graduate students were advised not to take his classes. He was given the most cramped and least attractive faculty office despite his senior rank and was subjected to verbal harassment from university police. After serving for many years as a tenured senior faculty member of Queens College, CUNY, noted author and political analyst John Gerassi was moved to voice his displeasure at the treatment he had been accorded, including the case of my noncandidacy. In a letter (May 15, 1994) to his department colleagues, he wrote:

> I have never been asked to participate in anything meaningful in this department. For example, I have never been asked to be an adviser to graduates or undergraduates or [anyone else]. . . . Now since my colleagues tell me they like me, and I assume that they are not saying that just to humor me, the reason must be political. Indeed, I remember years ago when I informed my colleagues that a friend of mine who was nationally known, in fact internationally respected, Michael Parenti, who would be a great draw because of his reputation, was available for a job (at a time when the department was actually trying to fill a line), I was quickly informed that he would not be considered no matter what, and I was told in effect to stay out of department business.

Gerassi concluded on an ironic note: "If nothing else, may I respectfully request that while all decisions may be made by a small group of my colleagues behind closed doors, do, please, let us know what those decisions are."

The only radical to receive tenure in the department of philosophy in the 1970s at the University of Vermont was Will Miller, a
popular teacher, published author, and political activist. Though he
prevailed in his battle for tenure, Miller was made to pay for it. He
was denied promotion and has remained an assistant professor for
twenty-five years with a salary frozen for most of that time at below
the entry level of the lowest paid faculty member. He was pushed
out of all courses required by philosophy majors. He was passed
over for sabbatical for thirteen years and finally received a one-
semester leave only after threatening court action. And he was per-
petually passed over for reduced teaching load, a consideration
regularly granted to his departmental colleagues on a rotation basis.

The Myth of the Radical Campus

Those who control the institutions of higher learning in the United
States should want the same good things for students that they so
passionately advocate for the denizens of "totalitarian" countries,
namely the opportunity to hear, study, express, and support (or reject)
iconoclastic, antiestablishment views in their media and educational
institutions without fear of reprisal. Instead, it is a rare radical
scholar who has not encountered serious difficulties when seeking
employment or tenure, regardless of his or her qualifications.

Conservatives believe otherwise. They see academia as permeated with leftism, not surprisingly since they describe as "left" anyone to the left of themselves, including mainstream centrists and
"moderates." To be sure, campus activism did not pass away with
the sixties. In the years since then, protests have arisen against the
university's corporate investments in an apartheid-ruled South
Africa, the nuclear arms race, U.S. involvement in Central America,
the U.S. invasion of Panama, and the U.S. massacre of Iraq. There
have been campus demonstrations in support of women's studies

and multiculturalism, and against racism, sexism, and Eurocentric biases in the curriculum.

Such protests have been relentlessly attacked by the corporate-owned media as "politically correct McCarthyism." Thus the attempts to fight reactionism are themselves branded as reactionism by slippery conservatives such as Nat Hentoff, William F. Buckley, and others too numerous to mention, who suddenly emerged as defenders of diversity, insisting that sexists, racists, and fascists should be free to express their venom but that their opponents are not free to denounce them for doing so.

With unspoiled ethnocentrism, the novelist Saul Bellow denigrated preliterate societies by asking, "Who is the Tolstoy of the Zulus? The Proust of the Papuans?" When criticized for his Eurocentric arrogance, Bellow bellowed in the *New York Times* (March 10, 1994): "We can't open our mouths without being denounced as racists, misogynists, supremacists, imperialists or fascists." Writers like Bellow, who enjoy every acclaim from conventional literary quarters and ready access to major media and leading universities, consider themselves unjustly put-upon when attempts are made to examine their unexamined biases. So is fostered the mythic image of a university dominated by feminists, lesbians, gays, Marxists, and African American militants. In this way are the roles of oppressor and oppressed reversed.

In dozens of TV opinion shows and numerous large-circulation publications across the nation, without any sense of irony, scores of conservative and neoliberal writers have complained of being silenced by the "politically correct." Their diatribes usually are little more than attacks upon socio-political views they find intolerable, ideas and histories they want to eradicate from college curricula—supposedly for the sake of preserving free speech and political tolerance. Through all these barrages, one never actually hears from the "politically correct" people who are supposedly dominating the universe of discourse.

Today there exists a national network of right-wing campus groups, with budgets ranging from $100,000 to $1 million. This network coordinates most conservative activities at schools around the nation. It funds over one hundred right-wing campus publications, reaching more than a million students (according to a study by the University Conversion Project, an organization dedicated to promoting peace activism and investigative journalism on campus). Conservative campus publications and organizations receive millions of dollars from the Sciafe Foundation, the Olin Foundation, Coors, and other wealthy, right-wing donors. The nearly complete lack of alternative funding from progressive groups belies the charge that political communication in academia is dominated by left-wingers.

In sum, viewpoints that arouse little controversy are considered neutral and objective when more often they are merely ideologically conventional. Studies that implicitly share the normative perspective of the dominant poltico-economic system are assumed to represent a value-free empiricism, a researching of the world "as it is." Accusations of partisanship hurled by the ivy-tower guardians are themselves intensely partisan, being leveled against those who challenge, but rarely against those who reinforce the prevailing orthodoxies. Most textbooks on U.S. government and U.S. foreign affairs propagate conventional biases in the guise of political verities, overlooking or denying the undemocratic enormities of class power and imperialism.

By accepting the empire on its own terms, then denying its existence and all the difficult questions it raises, many academics believe they have achieved a scholarly detachment from the turmoil of reality. And in a way they have.

CHAPTER 11

REAL ALTERNATIVES

In February 1991, while attending the National Grocers' Association, President Bush visited a model supermarket. When taken to the checkout counter and shown how to pass a couple of items over the scanner, he excitedly voiced his admiration for this "new technology." It was evident he had not visited a supermarket in years, if ever.

The incident is emblematic of the hidden class dimensions of our policy process. People who never set foot in a supermarket and never have to worry over a food budget make public policies for people who have to count every penny. Health policy is formulated by people who never have to sit for hours in a public clinic. Transportation policy is made by people who never have to wait for a bus or search for a parking space. Our education system is legislated by people who have never had to send their children or grandchildren to public schools. Our daycare policy is devised by people who have au pairs and nannies. Public recreational policy is in the hands of people who vacation on private country estates and never have to visit a crowded, polluted municipal beach. And occupational safety laws are written by people who have never been inside a factory or gone down into a mine.

"Moderate Alternative"

The "moderate" Democrats led by President Bill Clinton, who acceded to the White House in 1993, have proven about as faithful in their service to corporate America as their Republican predecessors. During his first two years in office, Clinton repeatedly noted that economic recovery "must come through the private sector." He fought like a lion for the North American Free Trade Agreement (NAFTA) and the General Agreement on Tariffs and Trade (GATT), both of which bypass the gains made in environmental, consumer, and labor protections—by circumventing the sovereign power of the nation-states themselves, bestowing upon unelected secret international tribunals the right to set standards for investments, thereby circumventing popular sovereignty.

In addition, the Clinton administration has done next to nothing about the environmental crisis, nothing about putting the nation's transportation systems on an ecologically sane course, nothing in regard to developing alternative energy sources. It has made no real changes in foreign policy, offering little support to democratic forces in the Third World, while continuing to prop up murderous anti-democrats such as Jonas Savimbi in Angola. The Clinton administration has given full backing to the CIA and its covert actions throughout the world and to the global military empire, its gargantuan budget and grandiose goals. When it comes to empire at home and abroad, a change in political party brings little change in state policy. U.S. imperialism remains an unexamined, unchallenged, and largely unperceived phenomenon in this country.

In a few limited ways Clinton has attempted to deal with the wreckage caused by the Reagan-Bush years. He did introduce a $21 billion expansion of tax credits for low-wage workers and created some new housing, job training, and community development programs. While grossly inadequate in scope, these initiatives represented a departure from the punitive policies of his predecessors. For the most part, however, in regard to policies of empire and republic, the Clinton administration manifested a continuity with previous ones that is no less dismaying for being expected.

The ruling politico-economic elites conveniently believe that the environment is doing just fine, certainly on their estates, resorts, and ranches. They dislike what they think are the overheated jeremiads of the environmentalists, who call for the kind of regulations that limit the prerogatives of industrial capital. They equate the well-being of their class and their investments with the national interest, and see the poor and the working multitudes as deserving of lesser consideration because they supposedly contribute so little.

Fundamental reform is so difficult because it does not serve the powers that be. But it should be no mystery what needs to be done to improve our economy and the life conditions of our people. Consider the following agenda.

Military Spending and Peacetime Conversion

The interests of the republic should no longer be sacrificed to the interests of the empire. The military spending binge of the last fourteen years is the major cause of the nation's $4 trillion national debt, runaway deficits, decaying infrastructure, and crushing tax burden. It has transformed the United States from the world's biggest lender into the world's biggest spender and debtor.

To save a trillion dollars over the next decade, we should cut the bloated, wasteful Pentagon budget by two-thirds within a few years. To save additional billions each year and minimize the enormous damage done to the environment, the U.S. government should stop all nuclear tests, including underground ones, and wage a diplomatic offensive for a nuclear-free world. It could shut down almost all of its hundreds of military bases abroad and stop playing the self-appointed, global guardian who monitors everyone else's behavior on behalf of the free market. "Power Projection" forces, the Navy's carrier battle groups, the U.S. Central Command (formerly the Rapid Deployment Force) and other forces used for armed interventions abroad could all be eliminated with no danger to our national security. Each of these cuts would save billions of dollars without putting the United States in any danger from abroad.

Eliminate the manned space program, a $30 billion boondoggle whose major contribution has been to wreak destruction upon the ozone layer. Eliminate the elaborate and expensive missile defense systems that are being developed and maintained to fight a total war against a superpower that no longer exists.

The depressive economic effects of ridding ourselves of a war economy could be mitigated by embarking upon a massive conversion to a peace economy, putting the monies saved from the military budget (the "peace dividend") into domestic needs. Millions of productive new jobs can be created if government invested peace dividend funds in human needs and municipal services, retraining displaced defense-industry workers for more productive and more socially useful jobs. The shift away from war spending would improve our quality of life and lead to a healthier overall economy.

The National Security State

Congress should abolish the CIA or drastically cut its budget and that of other national security agencies. Their mandates should be limited to intelligence gathering. Prohibit their subversive and violent covert actions against Third World social movements, and impeach those intelligence agency officers who fail to obey the lawful limits imposed on them and who continue to maintain links with organized crime. The power of the executive to act with criminally violent effect against various peoples, including our own, should be exposed, challenged, and stopped. The Freedom of Information Act should be enforced instead of undermined by those who say they have nothing to hide, then try to hide almost everything they do.

End U.S.-sponsored counterinsurgency wars against the poor of the world. Eliminate all foreign aid to regimes engaged in human rights violations against their own peoples. The billions of U.S. tax dollars that flow into the Swiss bank accounts of foreign autocrats could be better spent on human services at home. Lift the trade and travel bans imposed on Cuba and other countries that have dared to deviate from the free-market orthodoxy.[1]

Electoral Reform

Only the government can rein in the state. But to attain a more democratic government, we need to curb the power of the moneyed interests and lobbyists. All candidates, including minor-party ones, should be provided with public campaign financing. In addition, a strict cap should be placed on campaign spending for all candidates and supporters, with no loopholes allowed. These various measures will greatly reduce the power of money to preselect candidates and prefigure electoral results.

The various states should institute proportional representation so that every vote will count and major parties will no longer dominate

---

1. To effect these goals more pressure must be brought to bear on Washington. For the better part of a decade, tens of thousands of U.S. supporters of the Sandinista revolution did almost nothing in the way of launching an anti-interventionist political offensive within the United States because they were too busy going down to Nicaragua to experience the revolution firsthand. Likewise, in regard to Cuba; many advocates of a change in U.S. policy toward that country have been expending most of their time and energy organizing caravans to Cuba, rather than directing their energies and protests at the policymakers in Washington.

the legislature with artificially inflated majorities. Also needed is a standard federal electoral law allowing easy ballot access for third parties and independents.[2]

The media need to be democratized. The airwaves are the property of the people of the United States. As part of their public-service licensing requirements, television and radio stations should be required to give—free of charge—equal public air time to *all* political viewpoints, including dissident and radical ones, not only during election time but throughout the year. Only then can the present imperialist orthodoxy be challenged before mass audiences.

Tax Reform and Labor Law

Reintroduce the progressive income tax for rich individuals and corporations—without the many loopholes and deductions that still exist. Strengthen the inheritance tax and introduce a tax on accumulated wealth rather than on income alone. At the same time, give tax relief to the working poor and other low-income employees. Reduce the regressive Social Security tax; it produces a yearly $50 billion surplus that is shifted into the general budget to be spent on all sorts of things other than pensions for the elderly. Or increase Social Security payments to low-income elderly so that the surplus is spent on the people for whom it is intended.

Abolish antilabor laws like Taft-Hartley that make it so difficult for people to organize. Enforce government National Labor Relations Act protections on behalf of workers who now risk their jobs when they try to organize. Penalize employers who refuse to negotiate a contract after certification has been won. Repeal the restrictive "right to work" and "open shop" laws that undermine

---

2. For a more extended discussion of the existing electoral system and proportional representation, see my *Democracy for the Few,* 6th edition (New York: St. Martin's Press, 1995).

collective bargaining. And increase the minimum wage to a living wage level. Pass a law prohibiting the hiring of scab (permanent replacement) workers during a strike. Legislation along these lines was promised by the Clinton administration but never delivered. Clinton did nothing to push the bill prohibiting scab replacement to pass a threatened Senate filibuster in July 1994.

Americans are working harder and longer for less. In 1960 a college graduate with a mediocre academic record could earn enough to buy a three-bedroom house and a car and support a wife and three children. Today it takes two childless adults working full time to achieve a commensurate standard of living. While millions are overworked, millions have no work at all. We should initiate a six-hour workday or a four-day work week with no pay cut and no compulsory overtime.

Abolish NAFTA and GATT, international subterfuges that circumvent popular soveignty within all nations, endow multinational corporatism with omnipotence, and cripple protections for labor, consumers, independent producers, and the environment.

Agriculture and Ecology

Distribute to almost two million needy American farmers the billions of federal dollars now received by rich agribusiness firms. Encourage organic commercial farming with education and subsidies, and expeditiously phase out the use of pesticides, chemical fertilizers, and livestock hormones. Engage in a concerted effort at conservation and ecological restoration, including a massive cleanup of the land, air, and water. The most important issue that faces us is the survival of the planet's ecology. If that struggle fails, then everything else we do will be nothing more than rearranging the deck chairs on the *Titanic*.

Develop high-speed, mass-transit, magnetic monorail systems within and between cities for safe, swift, economical transportation, and develop electric and solar-powered vehicles to minimize the disastrous ecological effects of fossil fuels. Stanford Ovshinsky, president of Energy Conversion Devices, notes that a newly developed electric car now has a long driving range on a battery that lasts a lifetime. It uses environmentally safe materials and is easily manufactured, with operational costs that are far less than a gas-driven vehicle (*New York Times,* July 20, 1993). Phase out nuclear plants and initiate a long overdue crash program to develop thermal, hydro, tidal, and solar energy sources.

Health Care and Safety

Institute a single-payer health care system that provides comprehensive service to all and allows patients to go to the doctor of their choice as does the system in Canada and elsewhere. There is no reason to spend tens of billions more on health care insurance (as proposed by President Clinton) when we already expend more per capita than any other nation. The funds should go for medical treatment, not to giant insurance companies. Under single-payer, the insurance companies would be shut out of health-care profiteering.

Thousands of additional federal inspectors are needed for the various agencies responsible for the enforcement of occupational safety and consumer protection laws. "Where are we going to get the money to pay for all this?" one hears. The question is never asked in regard to the defense budget or the billions spent on business subsidies. We can get the additional funds from a more progressive tax system and from major cuts in business subsidies and military spending.

Fiscal Policy

Government could end deficit spending by taxing the financial class from whom it now borrows. It must stop bribing the rich with investment subsidies and other guarantees, and redirect capital investments towards not-for-profit public goals. We need to eliminate the multibillion-dollar welfare handouts to rich corporations and agribusiness. Let them try living up to their free-market rhetoric.

The national debt is a transfer payment from taxpayers to bondholders, from labor to capital, from average people to the wealthy. Like Latin American peasants, U.S. taxpayers will be sacrificing their standard of living for generations to pay off wealthy creditors. The right-wing policy of "borrow borrow, spend spend" ought to be ended. The national debt should be rescheduled, with full compensation slated for small Treasury bondholders and only partial compensation to large ones.

Social Justice and Jobs

End all racial and gender discriminatory practices in institutional settings, including the law and the courts themselves. Vigorously enforce the law to protect women from male abuse, children from adult abuse, and gays and minorities from hate crimes and police brutality. We need stronger federal efforts at fighting the violence perpetrated against abortion clinics and doctors by the fanatical advocates of compulsory pregnancy.

Initiate a massive federal employment program that would shift our public wealth away from empire and toward rebuilding the republic. In 1994, Representative Matthew Martinez (D-Calif.) introduced a $300 billion jobs bill to tackle the "highest rate of unemployment" since the 1930s. A Works Project Administration (WPA), more encompassing than the New Deal one, could employ people to reclaim the environment; build needed industries, affordable housing, and mass transportation systems; rebuild our parks, towns, cities, and a crumbling infrastructure; and provide services for the aged and infirm.

People could be put to work producing goods and services in competition with the private market. The New Deal's WPA engaged in the production of goods, including manufacturing clothes and mattresses for relief clients, surgical gowns for hospitals, and canned meat, fruits, and vegetables for the jobless poor. This kind of not-for-profit direct production to meet human needs brings in revenues to the government both in the sales of the goods and in taxes on the incomes of the new jobs created. Eliminated from the picture is private profit for those who live off the labor of others—which explains their fierce hostility toward government programs that engage in direct production.

The government subsidizes corporate interests at public expense. The policy changes listed above would dramatically reverse that flow, producing for human need rather than corporate greed, bringing us away from empire and closer to being a republic.

Needless to say, these reforms are easier said than done. They remain undone and largely untouched not because policymakers never thought of them. Rather it is that those who desire reform have not the power and those who have the power have not the desire for reform. If anything, they have a furious hostility toward those changes that democratize the economy and infringe upon their capital expropriations. What is needed is greater effort at organizing, educating, and agitating at every point of struggle, be it the workplace, the electoral system, the courts, the media, the college campus, or the streets. Also needed is greater unity and coalition building.

Class Warfare a Two-Way Street

The "greatness" of this country, as measured by its destructive military capacity, is a hollow standard around which to rally. The American people need something better than flag-waving hoopla and the easy slaughter of weaker peoples. They need a major transformation in public policy, away from empire and toward democracy. Many empires begin to decay when they are at the height of their military power. The martial state devours the resources that would otherwise go into developing the productive civilian sector. The rulers of this country preside over such an empire. They are able to interject U.S. power into every corner of the globe while unable to deal with basic problems at home.

Those of us who point out the class basis of imperialism are accused of preaching "class warfare." But top-down class warfare by the ruling elites against the middle and lower classes is what we already have as an everyday occurrence. It is only when the many begin to fight back against the few that class warfare is condemned by political and media elites.

Witness the case of Haiti, a country with generations of brutal class oppression, where the military and the rich have lived off the impoverished people and regularly made war upon them. Yet U.S. media and U.S. political leaders started using the term "class warfare" only when the people elected Jean-Bertrand Aristide as president, a populist reformer who attacked the crimes and privileges of the rich. So in other countries and in this one too: the moment the common populace begin to fight back, even peaceably and democratically, the moment democracy infringes upon powerful class interests, ruling-class leaders and their media mouthpieces denounce "class warfare." In the early 1990s in the United States, when some liberal Democrats started talking about taxing the rich, they were accused of class warfare. But when the rich advance their interests at our expense in ways too numerous to delineate here, it is called "national policy."

In his last State of the Union message, George Bush said that people who challenge the prerogatives of the rich are driven by envy and jealousy. I suspect it is not envy that most of us feel when we see somebody ride by in a Rolls Royce—and someone else sleeping in a doorway. We feel outrage. We just do not want to live in a society where millions must suffer acute privation and insecurity so that the very rich can maintain their lavish lifestyle. We do not want to change places with the opulent; we just want to get them off our backs. We want to stop the ruination of our society and environment by the conglomerates of wealth, those who engineer and finance national elections, who manage national policy and use crimes of state to eviscerate and trivialize democratic governance at home and abroad. If challenging and stopping such class power is class warfare, then let us have more of it.

We have another name for that struggle, a name borrowed from the ancient Greeks. When popular forces mobilize against the power of plutocracy, we call it democracy. Ultimately the worth of any system must be measured by a democratic standard. Does it serve the public interest or the private plunderer? Does it serve the needs of the many or the greed of the few? We need drastic reforms, revolutionary measures for a more viable and equitable society, one that is economically productive, ecologically sustainable, and socially just. Only that can bring about the end of empire and the triumph of democracy.

The "global economy" is another name for imperialism, and imperialism is a transnational form of capitalism. The essence of capitalism is to turn nature into commodities and commodities into capital. The live green earth is transformed into dead, gold bricks, with luxury items for the few and toxic slag heaps for the many. The glittering mansion overlooks a vast sprawl of shanty towns, wherein a desperate, demoralized humanity is kept in line with drugs, television, and armed force.

But every empire, triumphant in that heartless way, plants the seeds of its own destruction. The more successful its ruling class in devouring the wealth and resources of this and other lands, the more it undermines the base upon which it depends. Like some mythological beast that devours itself, the empire devours the republic, its human labor, and its natural environment. Alas, in this epoch, the self-ravagement is of such a magnitude that when the collapse comes, it may take down the entire ecosphere and all of us with it.

The history of imperialism is a history of unspeakable atrocities, mass slaughters, horrors, deceits, treacheries, and merciless oppression. It is enough to make one give up hope for the human race, both for its victims and victimizers. Today, the purveyors of capitalism ring the welkin with victorious pronouncements about a New World Order. Some of their faithful ideologues pontificate about "the end of history," concluding that the age-old struggle between haves and have-nots is being replaced by a monocentric, consensual, economic globalization. Yet peasants rise up in Mexico; masses mobilize in South Africa; workers and indigenous peoples organize in scores of countries to protect their lands and better their lives.

The head of the 1994 Zapatista rebellion in Chiapas, Mexico, Subcommander Marcos, recently responded to rumors that he was homosexual by issuing the following statement:

> Marcos is gay in San Francisco, Black in South Africa, an Asian in Europe, a Chicano in San Ysidro, an anarchist in Spain, a Palestinian in Israel, a Mayan Indian in the streets of San Cristobal, a gang member in Neza [a huge Mexico City slum], a rocker in the National University [where leftist folk music holds sway], a Jew in Germany, an ombudsman in the Defense Ministry, a communist in the post–Cold War era, an artist without gallery or portfolio, a pacifist in Bosnia, a housewife alone on Saturday night in any neighborhood in any city in Mexico, a striker in the CTM [the progovernment

labor federation that virtually opposes strikes], a reporter writing filler stories for the back pages, a single woman on the metro at 10 P.M., a peasant without land, an unemployed worker . . . an unhappy student, a dissident amid free-market economics, a writer without books or readers, and, of course, a Zapatista in the mountains of southeast Mexico.

So Marcos is a human being, any human being, in this world. Marcos is all the exploited, marginalized and oppressed minorities, resisting and saying, "Enough!"

Along with all its horrors and cruelties, the history of imperialism is a history of resistance and rebellion, coming sometimes in the most unexpected moments and places. Resistance to the self-devouring empire is not a chimera but an urgent necessity. Our best hope is that in times ahead, as in the past, when things look most hopeless, a new cry will be heard in the land and those who would be our masters are shaken from their pinnacles.

Not only must we love social justice more than personal gain, we also must realize that our greatest personal gain comes in the struggle for social justice. And we are most in touch with our own individual humanity when we stand close to all of humanity.

MICHAEL PARENTI is considered one of the nation's leading progressive thinkers. He received his Ph.D. in political science from Yale University in 1962, and has taught at a number of colleges and universities. His writings have been featured in scholarly journals, popular periodicals, and newspapers. Dr. Parenti lectures around the country on college campuses and before religious, labor, community, peace, and public interest groups. For audio tapes, contact Alternative Radio at ar@orci.com, and for video tapes, contact Ralph Cole at DemocracyU@aol.com. Dr. Parenti lives in Berkeley, California. His website is www.michaelparenti.org.

Printed in the USA
CPSIA information can be obtained
at www.ICGtesting.com
JSHW080539040524
62485JS00001B/12

9 780872 862982